Cooking School

INDIAN

Cooking School

INDIAN

Bring the flavors of India to life in your own kitchen!

This edition published in 2010
LOVE FOOD is an imprint of Parragon Books Ltd

Parragon
Queen Street House
4 Queen Street
Bath BA1 1HE, UK

ISBN: 978-1-4075-9478-1

Printed in China

Internal design by Pink Creative
Photography by Clive Streeter and Mike Cooper
Food Styling by Teresa Goldfinch, Sumi Glass, Carole Handslip, and Lincoln Jefferson
Introduction written by Christine McFadden

Notes for the Reader

This book uses imperial, metric, and US cup measurements. Follow the same units of measurement throughout; do not mix imperial and metric. All spoon measurements are level: teaspoons are assumed to be 5 ml, and tablespoons are assumed to be 15 ml. Unless otherwise stated, milk is assumed to be whole, eggs and individual vegetables, such as potatoes, are medium, and pepper is freshly ground black pepper.

The times given are an approximate guide only. Preparation times differ according to the techniques used by different people and the cooking times may also vary from those given as a result of the type of oven used. Optional ingredients, variations, or serving suggestions have not been included in the calculations.

Recipes using raw or very lightly cooked eggs should be avoided by infants, the elderly, pregnant women, convalescents, and anyone with a chronic condition. Pregnant and breastfeeding women are advised to avoid eating peanuts and peanut products. People with nut allergies should be aware that some of the prepared ingredients used in the recipes in this book may contain nuts. Always check the packaging before use.

Contents

Introduction

In India, the cooking and eating of food is taken seriously, with great appreciation and enjoyment. It is not eaten just to fill the stomach, but also to fine tune the body, both spiritually and physically, according to the ancient system of ayurvedic medicine. Indian cooks who maintain this long-held tradition carefully combine different seasonings and ingredients, adjusting them according to the health and temperament of family members, and also taking into account the season, time of the meal, and a host of other variables.

The cuisine is astonishingly varied and probably has a greater palette of flavors and seasonings than almost any other in the world. Indians love eating out and the range of eating places in city centers is wide. However, much of the best cooking takes place within the home, where recipes were traditionally handed down unwritten from generation to generation. Nowadays, more and more recipes are being recorded as food writers, cooking school owners, and chefs travel the world in search of inspiration.

Thanks to long-haul travel, the wide availability of exotic ingredients, and our fascination with spicy foods, Indian dishes have found a permanent place on the menu, in both the United States and Europe. Chicken Tikka Masala, although not strictly Indian, is a typical example, as are Lamb Rogan Josh and Tandoori Shrimp. The number of Indian take-out restaurants is increasing all the time, and the high level of cooking in modern Indian restaurants abroad is a far cry from what was available in the 1960s and 70s.

Indian Regional Cooking

With India's vast size and radical variations in topography and climate, the cuisine is highly regional. The diversity is most obvious in the contrast between the rich meat-based dishes of the northern states of Punjab, Kashmir, and Uttar Pradesh, and the vegetarian and fish-based cuisine of the south, where rice is the staple food.

Different religions, each with a strict dietary code, also have a strong influence. Muslims do not eat pork because it is considered unclean, nor are they supposed to drink alcohol. Hindus who are not vegetarians do not eat beef, nor do the Sikhs.

Invasions by colonizers have shaped the cuisine, too. Intrepid explorers from Portugal established Christian communities in southwest India and, as a result, the classic Pork Vindaloo found its way into Goan cuisine. In the days of the Raj, patient Indian cooks created mulligatawny soup for homesick British colonials, although soup was not previously part of their culinary repertoire.

The Indian Meal

In Indian homes, all the dishes are usually served together instead of as separate courses, although modern Indians sometimes serve soup as a first course. The dishes may be served in communal bowls, or each person may have his or her own thali—a large metal plate with individual bowls (katori) on it—or a huge banana leaf with portions of each dish arranged on it.

It is customary for Indians to use the fingertips of the right hand, instead of cutlery, to scoop up food, except possibly when entertaining Western guests. It is unacceptable to eat with the left hand because it is considered unclean.

A meal at home might consist of a meat or fish dish, one or two vegetable dishes, including legumes, such as lentils, and a large bowl of rice or freshly baked flat bread, with chutney or fresh relishes as an accompaniment. Vegetarian menus will include a greater choice of vegetables and legumes.

Meals are sometimes rounded off with a selection of chilled sliced fruit, although on special occasions a rich dessert, such as Shrikand, or a spicy rice pudding might be served.

What to Drink

Most Indians drink water with a meal instead of alcohol, which is usually enjoyed before the meal, accompanied by tasty snacks, such as Plantain Chips, deep-fried bhajis, or samosas. Where alcohol is forbidden, fruit juices and drinks made with fruit syrups are popular. Sweet or Salted Lassi, an iced drink made with lightly spiced yogurt, is the preferred drink in northern regions. A ginger syrup-flavored drink and lime soda pop, seasoned with sugar and black pepper, are served all over India and are particularly thirst quenching in the blistering heat.

Tips on Menu Planning

Planning an Indian meal is not so different from organizing a well-balanced, Western-style meal.

- Contrasting textures are important, as are a balance of rich and plain, hot and cooling foods.
- Always include bread, legumes, or rice.
- Pungent relishes and chutneys perk up the appetite and aid digestion.
- Include a yogurt-based sauce to tame the heat.
- For a special meal, add more meat and vegetable dishes, a larger selection of chutneys, and perhaps a salad.
- Chosen carefully, wine can accompany an Indian meal, but chilled beer or lager is a safer bet.

Cooking Techniques

Most Indian cooking is done on top of the stove instead of in the oven. The following basic techniques are not difficult but worth mastering.

Shallow-Frying

Less common in India than deep-frying, and mainly used for pancakes and certain breads. Use just enough clean vegetable oil or ghee to stop the food from sticking. The fat must be hot enough to gradually brown the food, but it should not be smoking or hazy.

Deep-Frying

Widely used in Indian cooking. For success, use clean peanut oil or ghee, both of which reach a high temperature without burning. The oil should be deep enough to cover the food and hot enough so that a morsel of uncooked food sizzles immediately.

Fry in small batches—crowding causes the temperature to drop, resulting in soggy food. Remove cooked food with tongs and drain well on paper towels. Always serve deep-fried foods piping hot.

Griddling

Griddling is a technique for cooking flat disks of whole wheat dough known as chapatis. Brush a tava (see equipment) with a little fat and place over medium heat. To test the temperature, sprinkle with a few drops of water, which should splatter when the tava is the correct heat.

Preparing and Cooking Spices

Once ground or crushed, spices quickly lose their distinctive flavors and aromas. Whole spices are a must if you want bright, zesty flavors. Indian cooks coax out maximum flavor by dry-frying whole spices without any oil. The spices are ready when they smell toasty and start to jump around the pan. Once toasted, spices can be ground to a paste with wet ingredients and used as a marinade, or to thicken sauces.

Tempering is another flavoring technique in which whole spices are quickly fried in a little hot oil or ghee before adding the rest of the ingredients.

Bhagar is similar to tempering and used to perk up bland food. Sizzled spices and oil are poured over just before serving. The dish is kept covered to retain all the fragrant aromas.

Cooking Equipment

Indian cooks use similar equipment to that found in Western kitchens. However, the following items will also come in handy.

Karahi

A bowl-shaped iron or steel pan with sloping walls, a rounded bottom, and two ear-shaped handles, used for deep-frying, shallow-frying, and simmering. A wide saucepan with flared sides or a Chinese wok will work just as well.

Mortar and Pestle

Every Indian kitchen has at least one mortar and pestle for grinding, crushing, or mashing spices, pastes, and other ingredients.

Spice Grinder

Indians use a special flat stone, but a small electric coffee grinder is more convenient. Remember to keep it solely for spices, because the flavor will permeate other foods.

Tandoor Oven

A traditional clay oven built into the ground. The food is slapped directly onto the clay walls or is speared on skewers that rest against the sides. The food cooks in the intense heat, and the juices drip onto the coals, producing the characteristic smoky flavor. The technique is almost impossible to re-create, but reasonable results can be achieved with a covered barbecue.

Tava

A slightly concave metal disk with a long handle used for cooking flat breads, such as chapatis.
A cast-iron grill or nonstick crêpe pan make good substitutes.

Velan

A slim rolling pin for making flat breads. It is thicker in the middle to help flatten any uneven dough.
A Western-style rolling pin can be used instead.

Ingredients

It's really easy nowadays to create authentic-tasting Indian food, thanks to the exciting range of exotic ingredients found in supermarkets and Asian food stores. The following are the most commonly used.

AMCHOOR

A powder with a sour flavor made from sun-dried, unripe mangoes.

ASAFETIDA

An odd-smelling yellow powder that adds an onionlike flavor to vegetable dishes.

BASMATI RICE

The long-grain fragrant rice used throughout India and known the world over.

CARDAMOM PODS

Green: Highly aromatic seeds in a small green or cream husk, used to flavor sweet and savory dishes.

Black: Large, brown, paper husk, with seeds that have a strong flavor; they are used sparingly in spice mixes.

CHILES

Widely used in Indian cuisine, either fresh when unripe and green or dried once red and ripe. Their heat ranges from mild to searingly hot.

CILANTRO

The leaves from the same plant that provides coriander seeds are used fresh as a distinctive flavoring and a garnish.

COCONUT

Creamed: An oily compressed block that is crumbled into rich curries and soups, available in Asian stores.

Flakes, dried: Use as a crunchy garnish, or to add texture to salads and fresh relishes.

Fresh: Sweet, nutty, crisp flesh, which can be grated and pressed to produce milk.

Milk, canned: Used instead of grated fresh coconut.

CORIANDER

The seeds from the same plant that provides fresh cilantro leaves are used freshly ground as a seasoning and in spice mixes.

CUMIN SEEDS

Strongly pronounced flavor, used whole or ground in spice mixes.

CURRY LEAVES

The leaves have a uniquely lemony, spicy, and slightly bitter flavor—not at all like curry. Available dried or fresh, the fresh leaves freeze well and can be stored for months.

FENUGREEK

Very hard, yellow seeds with a strong typically "Indian" flavor; also available as a powder.

GARAM MASALA

Originating from the cooler regions of northern India, a mix of spices that is believed to heat the body. There are many variations, used mainly for seasoning meat, chicken, and rice dishes.

GARLIC

Used extensively in curries, chopped finely and fried with onions, or processed to a paste.

Garlic paste: Peel and chop 1 head of garlic and blend to a paste with 2–3 tablespoons of water; it will keep for a week in the refrigerator.

GHEE

Butter that has been clarified to remove milk solids that would otherwise burn when heated. Used for all types of frying.

GINGER

Used extensively in many Indian dishes, chopped finely or processed to a paste.

Ginger paste: peel and chop about 3 oz/90 g ginger and blend to a paste in a food processor with 2–3 tablespoons of water; it will keep for a week in the refrigerator.

LEGUMES

Protein-rich lentils, dried peas (dal), and beans, used extensively throughout India.

MUSTARD OIL

Amber-colored oil made from pressed mustard seeds, briefly heated to a high temperature before use to tame the harsh mustardy flavor.

MUSTARD SEEDS

Reddish brown or black seeds with a mild nutty flavor, they are usually sizzled in oil at the start of cooking.

NIGELLA SEEDS

Also called kalonji, jet black seeds with a peppery flavor. Used in dhals, vegetable dishes, and sprinkled on naan.

PANEER

Homemade fresh cheese made from milk curdled with lemon juice. Cut into cubes and fried with spices as a snack, or added to curries, vegetable dishes, and salads.

PEPPERCORNS

Native to southern India and at one time the world's most important spice, used in spice mixes and most Indian dishes.

SAFFRON

Red-orange stamens of the *Crocus sativus* with a unique highly aromatic flavor. Always buy threads instead of the ground powder.

TAMARIND

A brown, pod-shaped fruit with a sour flavor, compressed into sticky blocks of pulp that are soaked in water. Also sold as a concentrate that can be spooned straight from the jar.

TURMERIC POWDER

Originating from a rhizome, but usually sold ground as a bright yellow powder with a musky, slightly bitter flavor; it is essential in curries.

YOGURT

Gives body and creamy texture to curries and kormas. Also served as a cooling sauce mixed with spices, chopped cucumber, or other vegetables.

Meat and Poultry

India boasts a fascinating choice of meat dishes, although the type of meat is often restricted by religion; Muslims do not eat pork, and nonvegetarian Hindus refrain from beef, as do the Sikhs. Lamb is probably the most frequently used meat on the menu because it is free from dietary restrictions. Chicken comes a close second; it is versatile, cheap, and as well suited to simmering in richly flavored sauces as it is to roasting and broiling. Chickens in India are usually free-range and with a flavor far superior to mass-produced birds.

Curries are, of course, the most famous of Indian meat and poultry dishes, but they are by no means the only dish in the Indian repertoire. There are delicately flavored creamy kormas,

dopiaza—a variation of korma cooked with plenty of onion—and plenty of delicious meat and rice or lentil combinations. There is also incendiary pork vindaloo cooked with vinegar, marinated and skewered lamb kebabs, tasty meatballs cooked in various sauces, and chicken roasted tandoori-style.

Even within this extensive choice, there are regional nuances that create a typical national dish with a distinctive flavor all of its own. South Indian curries, for example, are hot and fiery, while in Kashmir and Punjab in the north they are comparatively mild. Western or Goan meat dishes are slow-cooked, spicy, and thickened with coconut milk. In the East, sharp acidic flavors of tamarind, lime, or green mangoes are typical.

Lamb Pasanda

SERVES 4–6

1 lb 5 oz/600 g boneless shoulder or leg
 of lamb

2 tbsp garlic and ginger paste

4 tbsp ghee, vegetable oil, or peanut oil

3 large onions, chopped

1 fresh green chile, seeded and chopped

2 green cardamom pods, bruised

1 cinnamon stick, broken in half

2 tsp ground coriander

1 tsp ground cumin

1 tsp ground turmeric

generous 1 cup water

⅔ cup heavy cream

4 tbsp ground almonds

1½ tsp salt

1 tsp garam masala

paprika and toasted slivered almonds,
 to garnish

1. Cut the meat into thin slices, then place the slices between plastic wrap and pound with a meat mallet to make them even thinner. Put the lamb slices in a bowl, add the garlic and ginger paste, and rub well into the lamb. Cover and let marinate in the refrigerator for 2 hours.

2. Melt the ghee in a large skillet over medium–high heat. Add the onions and chile and sauté, stirring frequently, for 5–8 minutes, until golden brown.

3. Stir in the cardamom pods, cinnamon stick, ground coriander, cumin, and turmeric and continue stirring for 2 minutes, or until the spices are aromatic.

4. Add the meat to the skillet and cook, stirring occasionally, for about 5 minutes, until it is browned on all sides and the fat begins to separate. Stir in the water and bring to a boil, still stirring. Reduce the heat to its lowest setting, cover the skillet tightly, and simmer for 40 minutes, or until the meat is tender.

5. Mix the cream and ground almonds together in a bowl. Beat in 6 tablespoons of the hot cooking liquid from the skillet, then gradually beat this mixture back into the skillet. Stir in the salt and garam masala. Continue to simmer for an additional 5 minutes, uncovered, stirring occasionally.

6. Garnish with a sprinkling of paprika and slivered almonds and serve.

Lamb Rogan Josh

SERVES 4

1½ cups plain yogurt

½ tsp ground asafetida, dissolved in 2 tbsp water

1 lb 9 oz/700 g boneless leg of lamb, trimmed and cut into 2-inch/5-cm cubes

2 tomatoes, seeded and chopped

1 onion, chopped

2 tbsp ghee, vegetable oil, or peanut oil

1½ tbsp garlic and ginger paste

2 tbsp tomato paste

2 bay leaves

1 tbsp ground coriander

¼–1 tsp chili powder, ideally Kashmiri chili powder

½ tsp ground turmeric

1 tsp salt

½ tsp garam masala

1. Put the yogurt in a large bowl and stir in the dissolved asafetida. Add the lamb and use your hands to rub in all the marinade, then set aside for 30 minutes.

2. Meanwhile, put the tomatoes and onion in a food processor or blender and process until combined. Melt the ghee in a flameproof casserole or large skillet with a tight-fitting lid. Add the garlic and ginger paste and stir until the aromas are released.

3. Stir in the tomato mixture, tomato paste, bay leaves, coriander, chili powder, and turmeric, reduce the heat to low, and simmer, stirring occasionally, for 5–8 minutes.

4. Add the lamb and salt with any leftover marinade and stir for 2 minutes. Cover, reduce the heat to low, and simmer, stirring occasionally, for 30 minutes. The lamb should give off enough moisture to prevent it from catching on the bottom of the skillet, but if the sauce looks too dry, stir in a little water.

5. Sprinkle with the garam masala, re-cover the skillet, and continue simmering for 15–20 minutes, until the lamb is tender. Serve immediately.

Lamb Dhansak

SERVES 4–6

1 lb 9 oz/700 g boneless shoulder of lamb, trimmed and cut into 2-inch/5-cm cubes

1 tsp salt, plus extra to taste

1 tbsp garlic and ginger paste

5 green cardamom pods

1 cup yellow lentils (toor dal)

3½ oz/100 g pumpkin, peeled, seeded, and chopped

1 carrot, thinly sliced

1 fresh green chile, seeded and chopped

1 tsp fenugreek powder

scant 2½ cups water

1 large onion, thinly sliced

2 tbsp ghee, vegetable oil, or peanut oil

2 garlic cloves, crushed

chopped fresh cilantro, to garnish

DHANSAK MASALA

1 tsp garam masala

½ tsp ground coriander

½ tsp ground cumin

½ tsp chili powder

½ tsp ground turmeric

¼ tsp ground cardamom

¼ tsp ground cloves

1. Put the lamb and 1 teaspoon of salt in a large saucepan with enough water to cover and bring to a boil. Reduce the heat and simmer, skimming the surface as necessary until no more foam rises. Stir in the garlic and ginger paste and cardamom pods and continue simmering for a total of 30 minutes.

2. Meanwhile, put the lentils, pumpkin, carrot, chile, and fenugreek powder in a large heavy-bottom saucepan and pour over the water. Bring to a boil, stirring occasionally, then reduce the heat and simmer for 20–30 minutes, until the lentils and carrot are tender. Stir in a little extra water if the lentils look as though they will catch on the bottom of the pan.

3. Let the lentil mixture cool slightly, then pour it into a food processor or blender and process until a thick, smooth sauce forms.

4. While the lamb and lentils are cooking, put the onion in a bowl, sprinkle with 1 teaspoon of salt, and let stand for about 5 minutes to extract the moisture. Use your hands to squeeze out the moisture.

5. Melt the ghee in a flameproof casserole or large skillet with a tight-fitting lid over high heat. Add the onion and sauté, stirring, for 2 minutes. Remove one third of the onion and continue sautéing the rest for an additional 1–2 minutes, until golden brown. Remove the remaining onion immediately with a slotted spoon, as it will continue to darken as it cools.

6. Return the reserved onion to the casserole with the garlic. Stir in all the dhansak masala ingredients and cook for 2 minutes, stirring continuously. Add the cooked lamb and stir for an additional 2 minutes. Add the lentil sauce and simmer over medium heat to warm through, stirring and adding a little extra water, if needed. Adjust the seasoning, if necessary. Sprinkle with the remaining onion and garnish with cilantro.

Meatballs in Creamy Cashew Nut Sauce

SERVES 4

1 lb/450 g fresh lean ground lamb

1 tbsp thick plain yogurt

1 large egg, beaten

½ tsp ground cardamom

½ tsp ground nutmeg

½ tsp pepper

½ tsp dried mint

½ tsp salt, or to taste

1¼ cups water

1-inch/2.5-cm piece cinnamon stick

5 green cardamom pods

5 cloves

2 bay leaves

3 tbsp sunflower oil or olive oil

1 onion, finely chopped

2 tsp garlic paste

1 tsp ground ginger

1 tsp ground fennel seeds

½ tsp ground turmeric

½–1 tsp chili powder

generous 1 cup cashew nuts, soaked in ⅔ cup boiling water for 20 minutes

⅔ cup heavy cream

1 tbsp crushed pistachios, to garnish

1. Put the lamb into a bowl and add the yogurt, egg, cardamom, nutmeg, pepper, mint, and salt. Knead the meat until it is smooth and velvety. Chill for 30–40 minutes, then divide into quarters. Make five balls out of each quarter and roll them between your palms to make them smooth and neat.

2. Bring the cold water to a boil in a large saucepan and add all the whole spices and the bay leaves. Arrange the meatballs in a single layer, reduce the heat to medium, cover the pan, and cook for 12–15 minutes. Remove the meatballs, cover, and keep hot. Strain the spiced stock and set aside.

3. Wipe out the pan and add the oil. Place over medium heat and add the onion and garlic paste. Cook until the mixture begins to brown and add the ground ginger, fennel, turmeric, and chili powder. Stir-fry for 2–3 minutes, then add the strained stock and meatballs. Bring to a boil, reduce the heat to low, cover, and simmer for 10–12 minutes.

4. Meanwhile, process the cashew nuts to a paste in a blender and add to the meatball mixture, along with the cream. Simmer for an additional 5–6 minutes, then remove from the heat. Garnish with crushed pistachios and serve.

Marinated Lamb Brochettes

SERVES 4

1 lb 9 oz/700 g boned leg of lamb, cut into 1-inch/2.5-cm cubes

2 tbsp vinegar

½ tsp salt, or to taste

1 tbsp garlic paste

1 tbsp ginger paste

½ cup strained, whole-milk plain yogurt or Greek-style yogurt

1 tbsp chickpea flour

1 tsp ground cumin

1 tsp garam masala

½–1 tsp chili powder

½ tsp ground turmeric

3 tbsp olive oil or sunflower oil, plus 1 tbsp for brushing

½ red bell pepper, cut into 1-inch/2.5-cm pieces

½ green bell pepper, cut into 1-inch/2.5-cm pieces

8 shallots, halved

4 tbsp butter, melted

lemon wedges, for serving

1. Put the meat in a large nonmetallic bowl and add the vinegar, salt, and the garlic and ginger pastes. Mix together thoroughly, cover, and let marinate in the refrigerator for 30 minutes.

2. Put the yogurt and chickpea flour in a separate bowl and beat together with a fork until smooth. Add the cumin, garam masala, chili powder, turmeric, and oil and mix together thoroughly. Add the yogurt mixture to the marinated meat, then add the bell peppers and shallots and stir until well blended. Cover and let marinate in the refrigerator for 2–3 hours, or overnight. Return to room temperature before cooking.

3. Preheat the broiler to high. Line the broiler pan with a piece of foil. Brush the rack and 4 metal skewers with the oil.

4. Thread the marinated lamb, bell peppers, and shallots alternately onto the prepared skewers. Place the skewers on the prepared rack and cook for 4 minutes. Brush generously with half the melted butter and cook for an additional 2 minutes. Turn over and cook for 3–4 minutes. Brush with the remaining butter and cook for an additional 2 minutes.

5. Balance the brochettes over a large saucepan or skillet and let rest for 5–6 minutes before sliding the lamb, bell peppers, and shallots off the skewers with a knife. Serve with the lemon wedges.

Kashmiri Lamb Chops

SERVES 4

4 lamb chump chops or 8 chops
1¼ cups whole milk
1 tbsp ginger paste
½ tsp pepper
pinch of saffron threads, pounded
1½ tsp ground fennel seeds
1 tsp ground cumin
½ tsp chili powder
4 cloves

1-inch/2.5-cm piece cinnamon stick
4 green cardamom pods, bruised
1 tsp salt, or to taste
½ tsp garam masala
1 tbsp fresh mint leaves, chopped,
  or ½ tsp dried mint
1 tbsp chopped fresh cilantro leaves
mixed leaf salad, for serving

1. Remove the rind from the chops. Bring enough water to cover the chops to a boil in a medium saucepan. Add the chops, return to a boil, and cook for 2–3 minutes. Drain the chops, rinse, and drain again.

2. Put the drained chops into a large nonstick saucepan and add all the remaining ingredients, except the garam masala and herbs. Put the saucepan over medium heat and stir until the milk begins to bubble. Reduce the heat to low, cover, and cook for 30 minutes, turning the chops occasionally.

3. Remove from the heat. Using tongs, lift the chops out of the saucepan and shake the cooking liquid back into the saucepan. Strain the liquid and return to the saucepan with the chops. Cook over medium heat, turning frequently, for 7–8 minutes, until the liquid has evaporated and the chops are browned.

4. Sprinkle the garam masala evenly over the chops and add the mint and cilantro. Stir and cook for 1 minute. Serve immediately with a mixed salad.

Kheema Matar

SERVES 4–6

2 tbsp ghee, vegetable oil, or peanut oil

2 tsp cumin seeds

1 large onion, finely chopped

1 tbsp garlic and ginger paste

2 bay leaves

1 tsp mild, medium, or hot curry powder,
   to taste

2 tomatoes, seeded and chopped

1 tsp ground coriander

¼–½ tsp chili powder

¼ tsp ground turmeric

pinch of sugar

½ teaspoon salt

½ teaspoon pepper

1 lb 2 oz/500 g lean ground beef or lamb

2¼ cups frozen peas, straight from the freezer

1. Melt the ghee in a flameproof casserole or large skillet with a tight-fitting lid. Add the cumin seeds and cook, stirring, for 30 seconds, or until they start to crackle.

2. Stir in the onion, garlic and ginger paste, bay leaves, and curry powder and continue to stir-fry until the fat separates.

3. Stir in the tomatoes and cook for 1–2 minutes. Stir in the coriander, chili powder, turmeric, sugar, salt, and pepper and stir around for 30 seconds.

4. Add the beef and cook for 5 minutes, or until it is no longer pink, using a wooden spoon to break up the meat. Reduce the heat and simmer, stirring occasionally, for 10 minutes.

5. Add the peas and continue simmering for an additional 10–15 minutes, until the peas are thawed and hot. If there is too much liquid left in the casserole, increase the heat and let it bubble for a few minutes until it reduces.

Beef Madras

SERVES 4–6

1–2 dried red chiles

2 tsp ground coriander

2 tsp ground turmeric

1 tsp black mustard seeds

½ tsp ground ginger

¼ tsp pepper

1¼ cups coconut cream

4 tbsp ghee, vegetable oil, or peanut oil

2 onions, chopped

3 large garlic cloves, chopped

1 lb 9 oz/700 g lean braising beef, trimmed and cut into 2-inch/5-cm cubes

generous 1 cup beef stock, plus a little extra if necessary

lemon juice

salt

pappadams, to serve

1. Depending on how hot you want this dish to be, chop the chiles with or without any seeds. The more seeds you include, the hotter the dish will be. Put the chopped chiles and any seeds in a small bowl with the coriander, turmeric, mustard seeds, ginger, and pepper and stir in a little of the coconut cream to make a thin paste.

2. Melt the ghee in a flameproof casserole or large skillet with a tight-fitting lid over medium–high heat. Add the onions and garlic and cook for 5–8 minutes, stirring frequently, until the onions are golden brown. Add the spice paste and stir for 2 minutes, or until you can smell the aromas.

3. Add the meat and stock and bring to a boil. Reduce the heat to its lowest level, cover tightly, and simmer for 1½ hours, or until the beef is tender. Check occasionally that the meat isn't catching on the bottom of the casserole, and stir in a little extra water or stock, if necessary.

4. Uncover the casserole and stir in the remaining coconut cream with the lemon juice and salt to taste. Bring to a boil, stirring, then reduce the heat again and simmer, still uncovered, until the sauce reduces slightly. Serve with pappadams.

Balti Beef

SERVES 4–6

2 tbsp ghee, vegetable oil, or peanut oil

1 large onion, chopped

2 garlic cloves, crushed

2 large red bell peppers, seeded and chopped

1 lb 5 oz/600 g boneless beef, such as sirloin, thinly sliced

fresh cilantro sprigs, to garnish

Indian bread, to serve

BALTI SAUCE

2 tbsp ghee, vegetable oil, or peanut oil

2 large onions, chopped

1 tbsp garlic and ginger paste

14 oz/400 g canned chopped tomatoes

1 tsp ground paprika

½ tsp ground turmeric

½ tsp ground cumin

½ tsp ground coriander

¼ tsp chili powder

¼ tsp ground cardamom

1 bay leaf

salt and pepper

1. To make the balti sauce, melt the ghee in a wok or large skillet over medium–high heat. Add the onions and garlic and ginger paste and stir-fry for about 5 minutes, until the onions are golden brown. Stir in the tomatoes, then add the paprika, turmeric, cumin, coriander, chili powder, cardamom, bay leaf, and salt and pepper to taste. Bring to a boil, stirring, then reduce the heat and simmer for 20 minutes, stirring occasionally.

2. Let the sauce cool slightly, then remove the bay leaf and pour the mixture into a food processor or blender and process to a smooth sauce.

3. Wipe out the wok and return it to medium–high heat. Add the ghee and melt. Add the onion and garlic and stir-fry for 5–8 minutes, until golden brown. Add the bell peppers and continue stir-frying for 2 minutes.

4. Stir in the beef and continue stirring for 2 minutes, until it starts to turn brown. Add the balti sauce and bring to a boil. Reduce the heat and simmer for 5 minutes, or until the sauce slightly reduces again and the bell peppers are tender. Adjust the seasoning, if necessary. Garnish with cilantro sprigs and serve with Indian bread.

Pork with Cinnamon and Fenugreek

SERVES 4

1 tsp ground coriander

1 tsp ground cumin

1 tsp chili powder

1 tbsp dried fenugreek leaves

1 tsp ground fenugreek

⅔ cup plain yogurt

1 lb/450 g pork tenderloin, diced

4 tbsp ghee or vegetable oil

1 large onion, sliced

2-inch/5-cm piece fresh ginger, finely chopped

4 garlic cloves, finely chopped

1 cinnamon stick

6 green cardamom pods

6 whole cloves

2 bay leaves

¾ cup water

salt

1. Mix the coriander, cumin, chili powder, dried fenugreek, ground fenugreek, and yogurt together in a small bowl. Place the pork in a large, shallow nonmetallic dish and add the spice mixture, turning well to coat. Cover with plastic wrap and let marinate in the refrigerator for 30 minutes.

2. Melt the ghee in a large heavy-bottom saucepan. Cook the onion over low heat, stirring occasionally, for 5 minutes, or until softened. Add the ginger, garlic, cinnamon stick, cardamom pods, cloves, and bay leaves and cook, stirring continuously, for 2 minutes, or until the spices give off their aroma. Add the meat with its marinade and the water, and season to taste with salt. Bring to a boil, reduce the heat, cover, and let simmer for 30 minutes.

3. Transfer the meat mixture to a preheated wok or large heavy-bottom skillet and cook over low heat, stirring continuously, until dry and tender. If necessary, sprinkle occasionally with a little water to prevent the mixture from sticking to the wok. Serve immediately.

Pork Vindaloo

SERVES 4–6

4 tbsp mustard oil

2 large onions, finely chopped

6 bay leaves

6 cloves

6 garlic cloves, chopped

3 green cardamom pods, lightly cracked

1–2 small fresh red chiles, chopped

2 tbsp ground cumin

½ tsp salt

½ tsp ground turmeric

2 tbsp cider vinegar

2 tbsp water

1 tbsp tomato paste

1 lb 9 oz/700 g boneless shoulder of pork, trimmed and cut into 2-inch/5-cm cubes

1. Put the mustard oil in a large skillet or pan with a tight-fitting lid over high heat until it smokes. Turn off the heat and let the mustard oil cool completely.

2. Reheat the oil over medium–high heat. Add the onions and sauté, stirring frequently, for 5–8 minutes, until soft but not colored.

3. Add the bay leaves, cloves, garlic, cardamom pods, chiles, cumin, salt, turmeric, and 1 tablespoon of the vinegar to the onions and stir. Add the water, then cover the pan and simmer for about 1 minute, or until the water is absorbed and the fat separates.

4. Dissolve the tomato paste in the remaining vinegar, then stir it into the pan. Add the pork and stir around.

5. Add just enough water to cover the pork and bring to a boil. Reduce the heat to its lowest level, cover the pan tightly, and simmer for 40–60 minutes, until the pork is tender.

6. If too much liquid remains in the pan when the pork is tender, use a slotted spoon to remove the pork from the pan and boil the liquid until it reduces to the required amount. Return the pork to the pan to heat through, then transfer to warmed serving dishes and serve.

Chicken Tikka Masala

SERVES 4–6

14 oz/400 g canned chopped tomatoes

1¼ cups heavy cream

1 cooked tandoori chicken, cut into
   8 pieces

salt and pepper

fresh chopped cilantro, to garnish

cooked basmati rice, to serve

TIKKA MASALA

2 tbsp ghee, vegetable oil, or peanut oil

1 large garlic clove, finely chopped

1 fresh red chile, seeded and chopped

2 tsp ground cumin

2 tsp ground paprika

½ tsp salt

pepper

1. To make the tikka masala, melt the ghee in a large skillet with a lid over medium heat. Add the garlic and chile and stir-fry for 1 minute. Stir in the cumin, paprika, and salt and pepper to taste and continue stirring for about 30 seconds.

2. Stir the tomatoes and cream into the skillet. Reduce the heat to low and let the sauce simmer for about 10 minutes, stirring frequently, until it reduces and thickens.

3. Meanwhile, remove all the bones and any skin from the tandoori chicken pieces, then cut the meat into bite-size pieces.

4. Adjust the seasoning of the sauce, if necessary. Add the chicken pieces to the skillet, cover, and let simmer for 3–5 minutes, until the chicken is heated through. Garnish with cilantro and serve with cooked basmati rice.

Pistachio Chicken Korma

SERVES 4

¾ cup shelled pistachios

scant 1 cup boiling water

good pinch of saffron threads, pounded

2 tbsp hot milk

1 lb 9 oz/700 g skinless, boneless chicken
   breasts or thighs, cut into
   1-inch/2.5-cm cubes

1 tsp salt, or to taste

½ tsp pepper

juice of ½ lemon

4 tbsp ghee or unsalted butter

6 green cardamom pods

1 large onion, finely chopped

2 tsp garlic paste

2 tsp ginger paste

1 tbsp ground coriander

½ tsp chili powder

1¼ cups plain yogurt, whisked

⅔ cup light cream

2 tbsp rose water

6–8 white rose petals, washed, to garnish

cooked basmati rice and lemon wedges,
   to serve

1. Soak the pistachios in the boiling water in a heatproof bowl for 20 minutes. Meanwhile, soak the saffron in the hot milk.

2. Put the chicken in a nonmetallic bowl and add the salt, pepper, and lemon juice. Rub into the chicken, cover, and let marinate in the refrigerator for 30 minutes.

3. Melt the ghee in a medium heavy-bottom saucepan over low heat and add the cardamom pods. When they have puffed up, add the onion and increase the heat to medium. Cook, stirring frequently, for 8–9 minutes, until the onion is a pale golden color.

4. Add the garlic paste and ginger paste and cook, stirring frequently, for an additional 2–3 minutes. Add the coriander and chili powder and cook, stirring, for 30 seconds. Add the chicken, increase the heat to medium–high, and cook, stirring continuously, for 5–6 minutes, until it changes color.

5. Reduce the heat to low and add the yogurt and the saffron-and-milk mixture. Bring to a slow simmer, cover, and cook for 15 minutes. Stir halfway through to ensure that it does not stick to the bottom of the pan.

6. Meanwhile, put the pistachios and their soaking water in a blender or food processor and process until smooth. Add to the chicken mixture, followed by the cream. Cover and simmer, stirring occasionally, for an additional 15–20 minutes. Stir in the rose water and remove from the heat. Garnish with the rose petals and serve immediately with cooked basmati rice and lemon wedges.

Butter Chicken

SERVES 4–6

1 onion, chopped
1½ tbsp garlic and ginger paste
14 oz/400 g canned chopped tomatoes
¼–½ tsp chili powder
pinch of sugar
2 tbsp ghee, vegetable oil, or peanut oil
½ cup water
1 tbsp tomato paste
3 tbsp butter, cut into small pieces

½ tsp garam masala
½ tsp ground cumin
½ tsp ground coriander
8 cooked tandoori chicken pieces
4 tbsp heavy cream
salt and pepper
chopped cashew nuts and fresh cilantro sprigs, to garnish

1. Put the onion and the garlic and ginger paste in a food processor, blender, or spice grinder and process until a paste forms. Add the tomatoes, chili powder, sugar, and a pinch of salt and process again until blended.

2. Melt the ghee in a wok or large skillet over medium–high heat. Add the tomato mixture and water and stir in the tomato paste.

3. Bring the mixture to a boil, stirring, then reduce the heat to low and simmer for 5 minutes, stirring occasionally, until the sauce thickens.

4. Stir in half the butter, the garam masala, cumin, and coriander. Add the chicken pieces and stir until they are well coated. Simmer for about an additional 10 minutes, or until the chicken is hot. Taste and adjust the seasoning, if necessary.

5. Lightly beat the cream in a small bowl and stir in several tablespoons of the hot sauce, beating continuously. Stir the cream mixture into the tomato sauce, then add the remaining butter and stir until it melts. Garnish with the chopped cashew nuts and cilantro sprigs and serve straight from the wok.

Chicken Biryani

SERVES 4–5

⅓ cup whole-milk plain yogurt

1 tbsp garlic paste

1 tbsp ginger paste

1 lb 9 oz/700 g skinless, boneless chicken
  thighs

1 tbsp white poppy seeds

2 tsp coriander seeds

½ mace blade

2 bay leaves, torn into small pieces

½ tsp black peppercorns

1 tsp green cardamom seeds

1-inch/2.5-cm piece cinnamon stick, broken up

4 cloves

4 tbsp ghee or unsalted butter

1 large onion, finely sliced

1½ tsp salt, or to taste

RICE

pinch of saffron threads, pounded

2 tbsp hot milk

1½ tsp salt

2 cinnamon sticks, each 2 inches/5 cm long

3 star anise

2 bay leaves, crumbled

4 cloves

4 green cardamom pods, bruised

1 lb/450 g basmati rice, washed

TO GARNISH

2 tbsp sunflower oil

1 onion, finely sliced

1. Put the yogurt, garlic paste, and ginger paste into a bowl and beat together with a fork until thoroughly blended. Put the chicken in a nonmetallic bowl, add the yogurt mixture, and mix until well blended. Cover and let marinate in the refrigerator for 2 hours.

2. Grind the next eight ingredients to a fine powder in a coffee grinder and set aside. Melt the ghee over a medium heat in an ovenproof casserole, add the onion, and cook for 8–10 minutes, until a medium brown color. Reduce the heat, add the ground ingredients, and cook, stirring, for 2–3 minutes. Add the marinated chicken and salt and cook, stirring for 2 minutes. Turn off the heat and keep the chicken covered.

3. To make the rice, soak the saffron in the hot milk for 20 minutes. Preheat the oven to 350°F/180°C. Bring a large saucepan of water to a boil and add the salt and spices. Add the rice, return to a boil, and boil steadily for 2 minutes. Drain the rice, reserving the whole spices, and pile on top of the chicken. Pour the saffron and milk over the rice.

4. Soak a piece of wax paper large enough to cover the top of the rice fully in water and squeeze out the excess liquid. Lay on top of the rice. Soak a clean dish towel, wring out, and lay loosely on top of the wax paper. Cover the casserole with a piece of foil. It is important to cover the rice in this way to contain all the steam inside the casserole, because the biryani cooks entirely in the vapor created inside the casserole. Put the lid on top and cook in the center of the preheated oven for 1 hour. Turn off the oven and let the rice stand inside for 30 minutes.

5. Meanwhile, heat the oil for the garnish in a small saucepan over medium heat, add the onion, and cook, stirring, for 12–15 minutes, until browned.

6. Transfer the biryani to a serving dish and garnish with the fried onions.

Chicken Dopiaza

SERVES 4

1 lb 9 oz/700 g skinless, boneless chicken
    breasts or thighs
juice of ½ lemon
1 tsp salt, or to taste
5 tbsp sunflower oil or olive oil
2 large onions, coarsely chopped
5 large garlic cloves, coarsely chopped
1-inch/2.5-cm piece fresh ginger, coarsely
    chopped
2 tbsp plain yogurt
1-inch/2.5-cm piece cinnamon stick, halved
4 green cardamom pods, bruised
4 cloves

½ tsp black peppercorns
½ tsp ground turmeric
½–1 tsp chili powder
1 tsp ground coriander
4 tbsp canned crushed tomatoes
⅔ cup warm water
½ tsp sugar
8 shallots, halved
1 tsp garam masala
2 tbsp chopped fresh cilantro leaves
1 tomato, chopped
Indian bread, to serve

1. Cut the chicken into 1-inch/2.5-cm cubes and put in a nonmetallic bowl. Add the lemon juice and half the salt and rub well into the chicken. Cover and let marinate in the refrigerator for 20 minutes.

2. Heat 1 tablespoon of the oil in a small saucepan over medium heat, add the onions, garlic, and ginger, and cook, stirring frequently, for 4–5 minutes. Remove from the heat and let cool slightly. Transfer the ingredients to a blender or food processor, add the yogurt, and blend to a paste.

3. Heat 3 tablespoons of the remaining oil in a medium heavy-bottom saucepan over low heat, add the cinnamon stick, cardamom pods, cloves, and peppercorns, and cook, stirring, for 25–30 seconds. Add the processed ingredients, increase the heat to medium, and cook, stirring frequently, for 5 minutes.

4. Add the turmeric, chili powder, and coriander and cook, stirring, for 2 minutes. Add the tomatoes and cook, stirring, for 3 minutes. Increase the heat slightly, then add the marinated chicken and cook, stirring, until it changes color. Add the warm water, the remaining salt, and the sugar. Bring to a boil, then reduce the heat to low, cover, and cook for 10 minutes. Remove the lid and cook, uncovered, for an additional 10 minutes, or until the sauce thickens.

5. Meanwhile, heat the remaining oil in a small saucepan, add the shallots, and stir-fry until browned and separated. Add the garam masala and cook, stirring, for 30 seconds. Stir the shallot mixture into the curry and simmer for 2 minutes. Stir in the fresh cilantro and chopped tomato and remove from the heat. Serve immediately with Indian bread.

Chicken Jalfrezi

SERVES 4

1 lb 9 oz/700 g skinless, boneless chicken
    breasts or thighs

juice of ½ lemon

1 tsp salt, or to taste

5 tbsp sunflower oil or olive oil

1 large onion, finely chopped

2 tsp garlic paste

2 tsp ginger paste

½ tsp ground turmeric

1 tsp ground cumin

2 tsp ground coriander

½–1 tsp chili powder

5½ oz/150 g canned chopped tomatoes

⅔ cup warm water

1 large garlic clove, finely chopped

1 small or ½ large red bell pepper, seeded and
    cut into 1-inch/2.5-cm pieces

1 small or ½ large green bell pepper, seeded
    and cut into 1-inch/2.5-cm pieces

1 tsp garam masala

Indian bread or cooked basmati rice,
    to serve

1. Cut the chicken into 1-inch/2.5-cm cubes and put in a nonmetallic bowl. Add the lemon juice and half the salt and rub well into the chicken. Cover and let marinate in the refrigerator for 20 minutes.

2. Heat 4 tablespoons of the oil in a medium, heavy-bottom saucepan over medium heat. Add the onion and cook, stirring frequently, for 8–9 minutes, until lightly browned. Add the garlic paste and ginger paste and cook, stirring, for 3 minutes. Add the turmeric, cumin, coriander, and chili powder and cook, stirring, for 1 minute. Add the tomatoes and cook for 2–3 minutes, stirring frequently, until the oil separates from the spice paste.

3. Add the marinated chicken, increase the heat slightly, and cook, stirring, until it changes color. Add the warm water and bring to a boil. Reduce the heat, cover, and simmer for 25 minutes.

4. Heat the remaining oil in a small saucepan or skillet over low heat. Add the garlic and cook, stirring frequently, until browned. Add the bell peppers, increase the heat to medium, and stir-fry for 2 minutes, then stir in the garam masala. Fold the bell pepper mixture into the curry. Remove from the heat and serve immediately with Indian bread or cooked basmati rice.

Tandoori Chicken

SERVES 4

4 chicken pieces, about 8 oz/225 g each,
   skinned
juice of ½ lemon
½ tsp salt, or to taste
⅓ cup strained, whole-milk plain yogurt or
   Greek-style yogurt
3 tbsp heavy cream
1 tbsp chickpea flour
1 tbsp garlic paste
1 tbsp ginger paste

½–1 tsp chili powder
1 tsp ground coriander
½ tsp ground cumin
½ tsp garam masala
½ tsp ground turmeric
2 tbsp vegetable oil, for brushing
3 tbsp melted butter or olive oil
salad, to serve
lemon wedges, to garnish

1. Make 2–3 small incisions in each chicken piece and place in a large nonmetallic bowl. Rub in the lemon juice and salt, cover, and let marinate in the refrigerator for 20 minutes.

2. Meanwhile, put the yogurt in a separate bowl and add the cream and chickpea flour. Beat with a fork until well blended and smooth. Add all the remaining ingredients, except the oil and melted butter, and mix thoroughly. Pour over the chicken and rub in well. Cover and chill in the refrigerator for 4–6 hours, or overnight. Return to room temperature before cooking.

3. Preheat the broiler to high. Line a broiler pan with foil and brush the rack with oil. Using tongs, lift the chicken pieces out of the marinade and put on the prepared rack, reserving the remaining marinade. Cook the chicken for 4 minutes, then turn over and cook for an additional 4 minutes. Baste the chicken generously with the reserved marinade and cook for an additional 2 minutes on each side.

4. Brush the chicken with the melted butter and cook for 5–6 minutes, or until charred in patches. Turn over and baste with the remaining marinade. Cook for an additional 5–6 minutes, or until charred, tender, and the juices run clear when a skewer is inserted into the thickest part of the meat.

5. Transfer the chicken to a dish. Serve with salad and garnish with lemon wedges.

Silky Chicken Kebabs

SERVES 8

⅓ cup cashew nuts

2 tbsp light cream

1 egg

1 lb/450 g skinless, boneless chicken breasts,
coarsely chopped

½ tsp salt, or to taste

2 tsp garlic paste

2 tsp ginger paste

2 fresh green chiles, coarsely chopped (seeded
if you like)

1 cup fresh cilantro, including the tender stalks,
coarsely chopped

1 tsp garam masala

vegetable oil, for brushing

2 tbsp butter, melted

chutney, to serve

1. Put the cashew nuts in a heatproof bowl, cover with boiling water, and let soak for 20 minutes. Drain and put in a food processor. Add the cream and egg and process the ingredients to a coarse mixture.

2. Add all the remaining ingredients, except the oil and melted butter, and process until smooth. Transfer to a bowl, cover, and let chill in the refrigerator for 30 minutes.

3. Preheat the broiler to high. Brush the rack and 8 metal or presoaked wooden skewers lightly with oil. Have a bowl of cold water ready.

4. Divide the chilled mixture into 8 equal-size portions. Dip your hands into the bowl of cold water—this will stop the mixture from sticking to your fingers when you are molding it onto the skewers. Carefully mold each portion onto a skewer, forming it into a 6-inch/15-cm sausage shape. Arrange the kebabs on the prepared rack and cook for 4 minutes. Brush with half the melted butter and cook for an additional minute. Turn over and cook for 3 minutes. Baste with the remaining melted butter and cook for an additional 2 minutes.

5. Remove from the heat and let the kebabs rest for 5 minutes before sliding them off the skewers with a knife. Serve with chutney.

Fish and Seafood

With over 4,350 miles/7,000 km of coastline and numerous inland waterways, fish, seafood, and freshwater shellfish are main features on the Indian menu in certain areas. Coastal regions from north to south boast a vast array of fish and seafood, including some of the best lobster, shrimp, and crayfish. Goan Seafood Curry or Balti Fish Curry are particularly worth trying. Mussels are also good, especially when cooked Keralan style in a coconut sauce.

North of Bengal, toward Nepal, numerous rivers and streams flow down from the Himalayas. The icy water is clean and pure, and home to a great variety of lake and river fish. The Bengalis consider these superior to marine fish because the flavor is thought to be cleaner and fresher.

Sometimes fish are broiled whole on the spit, which produces a wonderful crispy skin and a moist and flaky interior. Firm-fleshed

fish may also be cut into chunks, sprinkled with a few spices, and brushed with oil, then cooked on skewers, such as Fish Tikka. Others are fried whole, sometimes coated in a spicy batter, or in fish and vegetable batter-coated fritters called pakoras.

Fish with a meaty texture, such as swordfish or cod, are gently braised in spicy sauces frequently flavored with coconut. Fish is also cooked in a rich tomato and chile sauce with crispy fried onions.

Other cooking methods for fish are baking, steaming, poaching, and roasting. Regardless of the method, all Indian fish dishes have that characteristic flavor that comes from a judicious mix of spices that enhance, but do not overwhelm, the delicate flavor of the fish.

Goan Fish Curry

SERVES 4

4 skinless salmon fillets, about 7 oz/200 g each

1 tsp salt, or to taste

1 tbsp lemon juice

3 tbsp sunflower oil or olive oil

1 large onion, finely chopped

2 tsp garlic paste

2 tsp ginger paste

½ tsp ground turmeric

1 tsp ground coriander

½ tsp ground cumin

½–1 tsp chili powder

generous 1 cup canned coconut milk

2–3 fresh green chiles, sliced lengthwise
  (seeded if you like)

2 tbsp cider vinegar or white wine vinegar

2 tbsp chopped fresh cilantro leaves

cooked basmati rice, to serve

1. Cut each salmon fillet in half and lay on a flat surface in a single layer. Sprinkle with half the salt and the lemon juice and rub in gently. Cover and let marinate in the refrigerator for 15–20 minutes.

2. Heat the oil in a skillet over medium heat, add the onion, and cook, stirring frequently to ensure even coloring, for 8–9 minutes, until a pale golden color.

3. Add the garlic and ginger pastes and cook, stirring, for 1 minute, then add the turmeric, coriander, cumin, and chili powder and cook, stirring, for 1 minute. Add the coconut milk, chiles, and vinegar, then the remaining salt, stir well, and simmer, uncovered, for 6–8 minutes.

4. Add the fish and cook gently for 5–6 minutes. Stir in the fresh cilantro and remove from the heat. Serve immediately with cooked basmati rice.

Fish Tikka

SERVES 4

pinch of saffron threads, pounded
1 tbsp hot milk
⅓ cup strained, whole-milk plain yogurt
1 tbsp garlic paste
1 tbsp ginger paste
1 tsp salt, or to taste
½ tsp granulated sugar
juice of ½ lemon
½–1 tsp chili powder

½ tsp garam masala
1 tsp ground fennel seeds
2 tsp chickpea flour
1 lb 10 oz/750 g salmon fillets, skinned and cut into 2-inch/5-cm cubes
3 tbsp olive oil, plus extra for brushing
sliced tomatoes and cucumber, to garnish
lemon wedges, to serve

1. Soak the pounded saffron in the hot milk for 10 minutes.

2. Put all the remaining ingredients, except the fish and oil, in a bowl and beat with a fork or a wire whisk until smooth. Stir in the saffron and milk, mix well, and add the fish cubes. Using a metal spoon, mix gently, turning the fish around until fully coated with the marinade. Cover and let marinate in the refrigerator for 2 hours. Return to room temperature before cooking.

3. Preheat the broiler to high. Brush the rack generously with oil and 8 metal skewers lightly with oil. Line the broiler pan with a piece of foil.

4. Thread the fish cubes onto the prepared skewers, leaving a narrow gap between each piece. Arrange on the prepared rack and cook for 3 minutes. Brush half the 3 tablespoons of oil over the kebabs and cook for an additional minute. Turn over and brush any remaining marinade over the fish. Cook for 3 minutes. Brush the remaining oil over the fish and cook for an additional 2 minutes, or until the fish is lightly charred.

5. Remove from the heat and let rest for 5 minutes. Garnish with tomatoes and cucumber and serve with lemon wedges for squeezing over.

Fish in Tomato and Chili Sauce with Fried Onion

SERVES 4

1 lb 9 oz/700 g tilapia fillets, cut into
2-inch/5-cm pieces

2 tbsp lemon juice

1 tsp salt, or to taste

1 tsp ground turmeric

4 tbsp sunflower oil or olive oil, plus extra
for shallow-frying

2 tsp sugar

1 large onion, finely chopped

2 tsp ginger paste

2 tsp garlic paste

½ tsp ground fennel seeds

1 tsp ground coriander

½–1 tsp chili powder

6 oz/175 g canned chopped tomatoes

1¼ cups warm water

2–3 tbsp chopped fresh cilantro leaves

cooked basmati rice, to serve

1. Lay the fish on a plate and gently rub in the lemon juice, half the salt, and half the turmeric. Set aside for 15–20 minutes.

2. Pour enough oil to cover the bottom of a skillet to a depth of about ½ inch/1 cm and place over medium–high heat. When the oil is hot, fry the fish in a single layer, until well browned on both sides. Drain on paper towels.

3. Heat the 4 tablespoons of oil in a medium saucepan over medium heat and add the sugar. Let it brown, watching it carefully because once it browns it will blacken quickly. Add the onion and cook for 5 minutes, until softened. Add the ginger and garlic pastes and cook for an additional 3–4 minutes.

4. Add the ground fennel seeds, coriander, chili powder, and the remaining turmeric. Cook for 1 minute, then add half the tomatoes. Cook until the tomato juice has evaporated, then add the remaining tomatoes. Cook, stirring, until the oil separates from the spice paste.

5. Pour in the warm water and add the remaining salt. Bring to a boil, then add the fish, stir gently, and reduce the heat to low. Cook, uncovered, for 5–6 minutes, then stir in half the cilantro leaves and remove from the heat. Sprinkle with the remaining cilantro and serve with cooked basmati rice.

Fish Korma

SERVES 4

1 lb 9 oz/700 g tilapia fillets, cut into 2-inch/5-cm pieces

1 tbsp lemon juice

1 tsp salt

½ cup unsalted cashew nuts

3 tbsp sunflower oil or olive oil

2-inch/5-cm piece cinnamon stick, halved

4 green cardamom pods, bruised

2 cloves

1 large onion, finely chopped

1–2 fresh green chiles, chopped (seeded if you like)

2 tsp ginger paste

2 tsp garlic paste

⅔ cup light cream

¼ cup plain yogurt

¼ tsp ground turmeric

½ tsp sugar

1 tbsp toasted slivered almonds, to garnish

Indian bread, to serve

1. Place the fish on a large plate and gently rub in the lemon juice and ½ teaspoon of the salt. Set aside for 20 minutes. Put the cashew nuts in a bowl, cover with boiling water, and let soak for 15 minutes.

2. Heat the oil in a wide, shallow saucepan over low heat and add the cinnamon, cardamom, and cloves. Let them sizzle for 30–40 seconds.

3. Add the onion, chiles, ginger paste, and garlic paste. Increase the heat slightly and cook, stirring frequently, for 9–10 minutes, until the onion is very soft.

4. Meanwhile, drain the cashew nuts and process them in a food processor or blender with the cream and yogurt.

5. Stir the turmeric into the onion mixture and add the processed ingredients, the remaining salt, and the sugar. Mix thoroughly and arrange the fish in the sauce in a single layer. Bring to a slow simmer, cover the pan, and cook for 5 minutes. Remove the lid and shake the pan gently from side to side. Spoon some of the sauce over the pieces of fish. Re-cover and cook for an additional 3–4 minutes.

6. Transfer to a serving dish and garnish with the slivered almonds. Serve with Indian bread.

Balti Fish Curry

SERVES 4–6

2 lb/900 g thick whitefish fillets, rinsed and cut into large chunks

2 bay leaves, torn

⅔ cup ghee, vegetable oil, or peanut oil

2 large onions, chopped

½ tbsp salt

⅔ cup water

chopped fresh cilantro, to garnish

Indian bread, to serve

MARINADE

½ tbsp garlic and ginger paste

1 fresh green chile, seeded and chopped

1 tsp ground coriander

1 tsp ground cumin

½ tsp ground turmeric

¼–½ tsp chili powder

1 tbsp water

salt

1. To make the marinade, mix the garlic and ginger paste, chile, coriander, cumin, turmeric, and chili powder together with salt to taste in a large bowl. Gradually stir in the water to form a thin paste. Add the fish chunks and smear with the marinade. Tuck the bay leaves underneath, cover, and let marinate in the refrigerator for at least 30 minutes, or up to 4 hours.

2. Remove the fish from the refrigerator 15 minutes in advance of cooking. Melt the ghee in a wok or large skillet over medium–high heat. Add the onions, sprinkle with the salt, and sauté, stirring frequently, for 8 minutes, or until they are soft and golden.

3. Gently add the fish with its marinade and the bay leaves to the wok and stir in the water. Bring to a boil, then immediately reduce the heat and cook the fish for 4–5 minutes, spooning the sauce over the fish and carefully moving the chunks around, until they are cooked through and the flesh flakes easily. Garnish with cilantro and serve with Indian bread.

Bengali-Style Fish

SERVES 4–6

1 tsp ground turmeric

1 tsp salt

2 lb 4 oz/1 kg monkfish or cod fillet, skinned
and cut into pieces

6 tbsp mustard oil

4 fresh green chiles

1 tsp finely chopped fresh ginger

1 tsp crushed garlic

2 onions, finely chopped

2 tomatoes, finely chopped

2 cups water

chopped fresh cilantro, to garnish

Indian bread, to serve

1. Mix the turmeric and salt together in a small bowl, then spoon the mixture over the fish pieces.

2. Heat the mustard oil in a large heavy-bottom skillet. Add the fish and cook until pale yellow. Remove the fish with a slotted spoon and set aside.

3. Place the chiles, ginger, garlic, onions, and tomatoes in a mortar and grind with a pestle to make a paste. Alternatively, place the ingredients in a food processor and process until smooth.

4. Transfer the spice paste to a clean skillet and dry-fry until golden brown.

5. Remove the skillet from the heat and place the fish pieces in the paste without breaking up the fish. Return the skillet to the heat, add the water, and cook over medium heat for 15–20 minutes. Transfer to a warmed serving dish, garnish with chopped cilantro, and serve with Indian bread.

Steamed Fish with Cilantro Chutney

SERVES 4

1 quantity of Cilantro Chutney (page 157)

1 large fresh banana leaf

vegetable oil or peanut oil, for brushing

4 white fish fillets, such as butterfish or sole, about 5 oz/140 g each

salt and pepper

lime or lemon wedges, to serve

1. Prepare the Cilantro Chutney at least 2 hours in advance to let the flavors blend.

2. Meanwhile, cut the banana leaf into 4 squares large enough to fold comfortably around the fish to make tight pockets.

3. Working with one piece of leaf at a time, very lightly rub the bottom with oil. Put one of the fish fillets in the center of the oiled side, flesh-side up. Spread one quarter of the cilantro chutney over the top and season to taste with salt and pepper.

4. Fold one side of the leaf over the fish, then fold the opposite side over. Turn the leaf so the folded edges are top and bottom. Fold the right-hand end of the leaf pocket into the center, then fold over the left-hand side. Trim the ends if the pocket becomes too bulky.

5. Use 2 wooden skewers to close the leaf pocket. Repeat with the remaining ingredients and banana leaf squares.

6. Place a steamer large enough to hold the pockets in a single layer over a pan of boiling water, without letting the water touch the fish. Add the fish, cover the pan, and steam for 15 minutes. Make sure the fish is cooked through and flakes easily.

7. Serve the fish pockets with lime or lemon wedges.

Butterfish in Chili Yogurt

SERVES 4

2 tbsp vegetable oil or peanut oil

1 large onion, sliced

1½-inch/4-cm piece fresh ginger, finely chopped

½ tsp salt

¼ tsp ground turmeric

pinch of ground cinnamon

pinch of ground cloves

generous ¾ cup plain yogurt

1 tbsp all-purpose flour

small pinch of chili powder

4 skinless butterfish fillets, about 5½ oz/150 g each, wiped dry

2 tbsp ghee, vegetable oil, or peanut oil

salt and pepper

2 fresh fat green chiles, seeded and finely chopped, to garnish

1. Heat the oil in a large skillet over medium–high heat. Add the onion and sauté, stirring, for 8 minutes, or until it is soft and dark golden brown. Add the ginger and stir around for an additional minute.

2. Stir in the salt, turmeric, cinnamon, and cloves and continue stirring for 30 seconds. Remove the pan from the heat and stir in the yogurt, a little at a time, beating constantly.

3. Transfer the yogurt mixture to a food processor or blender and process until a paste forms.

4. Season the flour with chili powder and salt and pepper to taste. Place it on a plate and lightly dust the fish fillets on both sides.

5. Melt the ghee in the wiped pan over medium–high heat. When it is bubbling, reduce the heat to medium and add the fish fillets in a single layer. Pan-fry for 2½ minutes, or until golden, then turn them over.

6. Continue cooking for an additional minute, then return the yogurt sauce to the pan and reheat, stirring. When the fillets flake easily and are cooked through and the sauce is hot, transfer to plates and sprinkle with the green chiles.

Fish Pakoras

SERVES 4

½ tsp salt

2 tbsp lemon juice or distilled white vinegar

1 lb 9 oz/700 g skinless white fish fillets, such as cod, halibut, or monkfish, rinsed, patted dry, and cut into large chunks

vegetable oil or peanut oil, for deep-frying

pepper

lemon wedges, to serve

BATTER

1 cup chickpea flour

seeds from 4 green cardamom pods

large pinch of ground turmeric

large pinch of baking soda

finely grated rind of 1 lemon

¾ cup water

salt and pepper

1. Combine the salt, lemon juice, and pepper to taste and rub all over the fish chunks, then set aside in a nonmetallic bowl and let stand for 20–30 minutes.

2. Meanwhile, to make the batter, put the chickpea flour in a bowl and stir in the seeds from the cardamom pods, the turmeric, baking soda, lemon rind, and salt and pepper to taste. Make a well in the center and gradually stir in the water until a thin batter forms, similar in consistency to light cream.

3. Gently stir the pieces of fish into the batter, being careful to avoid breaking them up.

4. Heat enough oil for deep-frying in a wok, deep-fat fryer, or large heavy-bottom pan to 350°F/180°C, or until a cube of bread browns in 30 seconds. Remove the fish pieces from the batter and let the excess batter drip back into the bowl. Without overcrowding the pan, drop fish pieces in the hot oil and cook for about 2½–3 minutes, until golden brown.

5. Use a slotted spoon to remove the fish pieces from the oil and drain on crumpled paper towels. Continue until all the fish is cooked, then serve hot with the lemon wedges.

Goan-Style Seafood Curry

SERVES 4–6

3 tbsp vegetable oil or peanut oil

1 tbsp black mustard seeds

12 fresh or 1 tbsp dried curry leaves

6 shallots, finely chopped

1 garlic clove, crushed

1 tsp ground turmeric

½ tsp ground coriander

¼–½ tsp chili powder

scant 3 cups coconut cream

1 lb 2 oz/500 g whitefish fillets, cut into large chunks

1 lb/450 g large shrimp, peeled and deveined

juice and finely grated rind of 1 lime

salt

1. Heat the oil in a wok or large skillet over high heat. Add the mustard seeds and stir them around for about 1 minute, or until they pop. Stir in the curry leaves.

2. Add the shallots and garlic and stir for about 5 minutes, or until the shallots are golden. Stir in the turmeric, coriander, and chili powder and continue stirring for about 30 seconds.

3. Add the coconut cream. Bring to a boil, then reduce the heat to medium and stir for about 2 minutes.

4. Reduce the heat to low, add the fish, and simmer for 1 minute, spooning the sauce over the fish and very gently spooning it around. Add the shrimp and continue to simmer for an additional 4–5 minutes, until the fish flakes easily and the shrimp turn pink and curl.

5. Add half the lime juice, then taste and add more lime juice and salt to taste. Sprinkle with the lime rind and serve.

Shrimp and Pineapple Tikka

SERVES 4

1 tsp cumin seeds
1 tsp coriander seeds
½ tsp fennel seeds
½ tsp yellow mustard seeds
¼ tsp fenugreek seeds
¼ tsp nigella seeds
pinch of chili powder

2 tbsp lemon or pineapple juice
12 jumbo shrimp, peeled, deveined, and tails left intact
12 bite-size wedges of fresh or well-drained canned pineapple
salt
chopped fresh cilantro, to garnish

1. If you are using wooden skewers for this rather than metal ones, place 4 skewers upright in a tall glass of water to soak for 20 minutes so they do not burn under the broiler.

2. Dry-roast the cumin, coriander, fennel, mustard, fenugreek, and nigella seeds in a hot skillet over high heat, stirring them around constantly, until you can smell the aroma of the spices. Immediately turn the spices out of the pan so they do not burn.

3. Put the spices in a spice grinder or mortar, add the chili powder and salt to taste, and grind to a fine powder. Transfer to a nonmetallic bowl and stir in the lemon juice.

4. Add the shrimp to the bowl and stir them around so they are well coated, then set aside to marinate for 10 minutes. Meanwhile, preheat the broiler to high.

5. Thread 3 shrimp and 3 pineapple wedges alternately onto each wooden or metal skewer. Broil about 4 inches/10 cm from the heat for 2 minutes on each side, brushing with any leftover marinade, until the shrimp turn pink and are cooked through.

6. Serve the shrimp and pineapple wedges on the skewers on a plate with plenty of cilantro sprinkled over.

Tandoori Shrimp

SERVES 4

4 tbsp plain yogurt

2 fresh green chiles, seeded and chopped

½ tbsp garlic and ginger paste

seeds from 4 green cardamom pods

2 tsp ground cumin

1 tsp tomato paste

¼ tsp ground turmeric

¼ tsp salt

pinch of chili powder, ideally Kashmiri chili powder

24 jumbo shrimp, thawed if frozen, peeled, deveined, and tails left intact

oil, for greasing

lemon or lime wedges, to serve

1. Put the yogurt, chiles, and garlic and ginger paste in a small food processor or spice grinder and process to a paste. Alternatively use a pestle and mortar. Transfer the paste to a large nonmetallic bowl and stir in the cardamom seeds, cumin, tomato paste, turmeric, salt, and chili powder.

2. Add the shrimp to the bowl and use your hands to make sure they are coated with the yogurt marinade. Cover the bowl with plastic wrap and chill for at least 30 minutes, or up to 4 hours.

3. When you are ready to cook, heat a large grill pan or skillet over high heat until a few drops of water "dance" when they hit the surface. Use crumpled paper towels or a pastry brush to grease the hot pan very lightly with oil.

4. Use tongs to lift the shrimp out of the marinade, letting the excess drip back into the bowl, then place the shrimp on the pan and cook for 2 minutes. Flip the shrimp over and cook for an additional 1–2 minutes, until they turn pink, curl, and are opaque all the way through when you cut one. Serve the shrimp immediately with lemon or lime wedges for squeezing over.

Shrimp Pooris

SERVES 6

2 tsp coriander seeds
½ tsp black peppercorns
1 large garlic clove, crushed
1 tsp ground turmeric
¼–½ tsp chili powder
½ tsp salt
3 tbsp ghee, vegetable oil, or peanut oil
1 onion, grated

1 lb 12 oz/800 g canned crushed tomatoes
pinch of sugar
1 lb 2 oz/500 g small, cooked, peeled shrimp, thawed if frozen
½ tsp garam masala, plus extra to garnish
6 Pooris, kept warm
chopped fresh cilantro, to garnish

1. Put the coriander seeds, peppercorns, garlic, turmeric, chili powder, and salt in a small food processor, spice grinder, or mortar and blend to a thick paste.

2. Melt the ghee in a wok or large skillet over medium–low heat. Add the paste and cook, stirring continuously, for about 30 seconds.

3. Add the grated onion and stir for an additional 30 seconds. Stir in the tomatoes and the sugar. Bring to a boil, stirring, and let bubble for 10 minutes, mashing the tomatoes against the side of the wok to break them down, or until reduced. Taste and add extra salt, if necessary.

4. Add the shrimp and sprinkle with the garam masala. When the shrimp are hot, arrange the hot pooris on plates and top each one with a portion of the shrimp. Sprinkle with the cilantro and garam masala and serve.

Mussels in Coconut Sauce

SERVES 4

2 lb 4 oz/1 kg mussels, scrubbed and
   debearded

3 tbsp ghee or vegetable oil

1 onion, finely chopped

1 tsp garlic paste

1 tsp ginger paste

1 tsp ground cumin

1 tsp ground coriander

½ tsp ground turmeric

pinch of salt

2½ cups canned coconut milk

chopped fresh cilantro, to garnish

1. Discard any mussels with broken shells and any that refuse to close when tapped with a knife. Set aside.

2. Heat the ghee in a large heavy-bottom skillet. Add the onion and cook over low heat, stirring occasionally, for 10 minutes, or until golden.

3. Add the garlic and ginger pastes and cook, stirring constantly, for 2 minutes. Add the cumin, ground coriander, turmeric, and salt and cook, stirring constantly, for an additional 2 minutes. Stir in the coconut milk and bring to a boil.

4. Add the mussels, cover, and cook for 5 minutes, or until the mussels have opened. Discard any mussels that remain closed. Transfer the mussels, with the coconut sauce, to a large warmed serving dish. Sprinkle with chopped cilantro and serve immediately.

Mussels with Mustard Seeds and Shallots

SERVES 4

4 lb 8 oz/2 kg mussels, scrubbed and
   debearded

3 tbsp vegetable oil or peanut oil

½ tbsp black mustard seeds

8 shallots, chopped

2 garlic cloves, crushed

2 tbsp distilled white vinegar

4 small fresh red chiles

1¼ cups coconut cream

10 fresh or 1 tbsp dried curry leaves

½ tsp ground turmeric

¼–½ tsp chili powder

salt

1. Discard any mussels with broken shells and any that refuse to close when tapped with a knife.
   Set aside.

2. Heat the oil in a wok or large skillet over medium–high heat. Add the mustard seeds and stir them
   around for 1 minute, or until they start to pop.

3. Add the shallots and garlic and cook, stirring frequently, for 3 minutes, or until they start to brown.
   Stir in the vinegar, whole chiles, coconut cream, curry leaves, turmeric, chili powder, and a pinch of
   salt and bring to a boil, stirring.

4. Reduce the heat to low. Add the mussels, cover the wok, and let the mussels simmer, shaking the
   wok frequently, for 3–4 minutes, or until they are all open. Discard any mussels that remain closed.
   Ladle the mussels into deep bowls, then taste the broth and add extra salt, if necessary. Spoon over
   the mussels and serve.

Vegetables and Legumes

Born of the centuries-old tradition of vegetarianism, Indian cooks weave their magic with vegetables and legumes, turning the simplest of fresh or dried produce into the most spectacular of feasts. Some of the cooking methods may be unfamiliar, but they result in snacks and meals that are both a pleasure to eat and nourishing to the mind and body. Popular dishes are vegetable curries and kormas, fritters and bhajis, and thick lentil-based soups called sambars. Potatoes are always popular, particularly with spinach or cauliflower. Green beans and potatoes are another favorite combination.

The culture of vegetarianism is most strong in the south, due mainly to the predominant Hindu religion, with its reverence for cows and its ideal of harmonizing the diet with the needs of the soul. Another more practical reason for the widespread uptake is that growing

vegetables is a more efficient and economic use of land than raising animals for food.

Legumes, such as chickpeas and lentils (dal), are an important source of protein in the vegetarian diet, especially when combined with other plant protein foods, such as rice (as in Kitchiri) or bread. A typical southern Indian vegetarian meal will usually consist of dal, two or three vegetable dishes, and a large dish of rice, with some pappadams, pickles, and chutney.

Also bear in mind the fact that meat in India is not always the nutritious and succulent product that we are used to in the West. It is expensive, too, and for these reasons must be heavily supplemented with legumes and vegetables to create the necessary balance of nutrients in the diet.

Vegetable Korma

SERVES 4

½ cup cashew nuts

¾ cup boiling water

good pinch of saffron threads, pounded

2 tbsp hot milk

1 head of cauliflower, divided into ½-inch/1-cm florets

4 oz/115 g green beans, cut into 1-inch/2.5-cm lengths

2 carrots, cut into 1-inch/2.5-cm sticks

4 tbsp sunflower oil or olive oil

1 large onion, finely chopped

2 tsp ginger paste

1–2 fresh green chiles, chopped (seeded if you like)

2 tsp ground coriander

½ tsp ground turmeric

6 tbsp warm water

1¾ cups vegetable stock

½ tsp salt, or to taste

9 oz/250 g young, waxy potatoes, boiled in their skins, cooled, and halved

2 tbsp light cream

2 tsp ghee or butter

1 tsp garam masala

¼ tsp grated nutmeg

1. Soak the cashew nuts in the boiling water in a heatproof bowl for 20 minutes. Meanwhile, soak the pounded saffron in the hot milk.

2. Blanch the vegetables in a saucepan of boiling salted water, then drain and immediately plunge in cold water. The cauliflower and green beans should each be blanched for 3 minutes; the carrots will need 4 minutes.

3. Heat the oil in a medium, heavy-bottom saucepan over medium heat. Add the onion, ginger paste, and chiles and cook, stirring frequently, for 5–6 minutes, until the onion is softened. Add the coriander and turmeric and cook, stirring, for 1 minute. Add half the warm water and cook for 2–3 minutes. Repeat this process with the remaining warm water, then cook, stirring frequently, for 2–3 minutes, or until the oil separates from the spice paste.

4. Add the stock, saffron and milk mixture, and salt, and bring to a boil. Drain the vegetables, add to the saucepan with the potatoes, and return to a boil. Reduce the heat to low and simmer for 2–3 minutes.

5. Meanwhile, put the cashew nuts and their soaking water in a food processor and process until well blended. Add to the korma, then stir in the cream. Reduce the heat to low.

6. Melt the ghee in a small saucepan over low heat. Add the garam masala and nutmeg and sizzle gently for 20–25 seconds. Fold the spiced butter into the korma. Remove from the heat and serve.

Cumin-Scented Eggplant and Potato Curry

SERVES 4

1 large eggplant, about 12 oz/350 g

8 oz/225 g potatoes, boiled in their skins and cooled

3 tbsp sunflower oil or olive oil

½ tsp black mustard seeds

½ tsp nigella seeds

½ tsp fennel seeds

1 onion, finely chopped

1-inch/2.5-cm piece fresh ginger, grated

2 fresh green chiles, chopped (seeded if you like)

½ tsp ground cumin

1 tsp ground coriander

1 tsp ground turmeric

½ tsp chili powder

1 tbsp tomato paste

scant 2 cups warm water

1 tsp salt, or to taste

½ tsp garam masala

2 tbsp chopped fresh cilantro leaves

Indian bread, to serve

1. Quarter the eggplant lengthwise and cut the stem end of each quarter into 2-inch/5-cm pieces. Halve the remaining part of the quarters and cut into 2-inch/5-cm pieces. Soak the eggplant pieces in cold water.

2. Peel the potatoes and cut into 2-inch/5-cm cubes. Heat the oil in a large saucepan over medium heat. When hot, add the mustard seeds and, as soon as they start popping, add the nigella seeds and fennel seeds.

3. Add the onion, ginger, and chiles and cook for 7–8 minutes, until the mixture begins to brown.

4. Add the cumin, coriander, turmeric, and chili powder. Cook for about 1 minute, then add the tomato paste. Cook for an additional 1 minute, then pour in the warm water and add the salt and drained eggplant. Bring to a boil and cook over medium heat for 8–10 minutes, stirring frequently to make sure that the eggplant cooks evenly. At the start of cooking, the eggplant will float, but once it soaks up the liquid it will sink quickly. As soon as the eggplant sinks, add the potatoes and cook for 2–3 minutes, stirring.

5. Stir in the garam masala and chopped cilantro and remove from the heat. Serve with Indian bread.

Green Bean and Potato Curry

SERVES 6

1¼ cups vegetable oil

1 tsp white cumin seeds

1 tsp mixed mustard and onion seeds

4 dried red chiles

3 fresh tomatoes, sliced

1 tsp salt

1 tsp fresh ginger, finely chopped

1 tsp crushed fresh garlic

1 tsp chili powder

7 oz/200 g green beans, diagonally sliced into 1-inch/2.5-cm pieces

2 potatoes, peeled and diced

1¼ cups water

TO GARNISH

fresh cilantro, chopped and green chiles, finely sliced, to garnish

1. Heat the oil in a large, heavy-bottom pan. Add the white cumin seeds, mustard and onion seeds, and dried red chiles, stirring well.

2. Add the tomatoes to the pan and stir-fry the mixture for 3–5 minutes.

3. Mix the salt, ginger, garlic, and chili powder together in a bowl and spoon into the saucepan. Blend the whole mixture together.

4. Add the green beans and potatoes to the pan and stir-fry for 5 minutes.

5. Add the water to the pan, reduce the heat, and let simmer for 10–15 minutes, stirring occasionally. Transfer to a warmed serving dish, garnish with chopped cilantro and green chiles, and serve.

Vegetable Sambar

SERVES 6

1 lb 12 oz/800 g canned tomatoes

2 tbsp dry unsweetened coconut

2 tbsp lemon juice

1 tbsp yellow mustard seeds

scant ¼ cup raw or brown sugar

2 tbsp ghee or vegetable oil

2 onions, sliced

4 cardamom pods, lightly crushed

6 curry leaves, plus extra to garnish

2 tsp ground coriander

2 tsp ground cumin

1 tsp ground turmeric

1 tsp ginger paste

1 cup toor dal (yellow lentils)

1 lb/450 g sweet potatoes, cut into chunks

2 lb/900 g potatoes, cut into chunks

2 carrots, sliced

2 zucchini, cut into chunks

1 eggplant, cut into chunks

salt

1. Place the tomatoes and their can juices, coconut, 1 tablespoon of the lemon juice, the mustard seeds, and sugar in a food processor or blender and process until smooth.

2. Heat the ghee in a large, heavy-bottom pan. Add the onion and cook over low heat, stirring occasionally, for 10 minutes, or until golden. Add the cardamoms, curry leaves, coriander, cumin, turmeric, and ginger paste and cook, stirring constantly, for 1–2 minutes, or until the spices give off their aroma.

3. Stir in the tomato mixture and dal and bring to a boil. Reduce the heat, cover, and let simmer for 10 minutes.

4. Add the sweet potatoes, potatoes, and carrots, re-cover the pan, and let simmer for an additional 15 minutes. Add the zucchini, eggplant, and remaining lemon juice, add salt to taste, re-cover, and let simmer for an additional 10–15 minutes, or until the vegetables are tender. Serve garnished with curry leaves.

Spinach and Paneer

SERVES 4

6 tbsp ghee, vegetable oil, or peanut oil

12 oz/350 g paneer, cut into ½-inch/1-cm pieces

1½ tbsp garlic and ginger paste

1 fresh green chile, seeded if you like, and chopped

4 tbsp water

1 onion, finely chopped

1 lb 5 oz/600 g fresh spinach leaves, any thick stems removed and rinsed

¼ tsp salt

¼ tsp garam masala

4 tbsp heavy cream

lemon wedges, to serve

1. Melt the ghee in a flameproof casserole or large skillet with a tight-fitting lid over medium–high heat. Add as many paneer pieces as will fit in a single layer without overcrowding the casserole and pan-fry for about 5 minutes, until golden brown on all sides. Use a slotted spoon to remove the paneer and drain it on crumpled paper towels. Continue, adding a little extra ghee, if necessary, until all the paneer is cooked.

2. Put the garlic and ginger paste and chile in a spice grinder or mortar and grind until a thick paste forms. Add the water and blend again.

3. Reheat the casserole with the ghee. Stir in the onion with the garlic and ginger paste mixture and sauté, stirring frequently, for 5–8 minutes, until the onion is soft, but not brown.

4. Add the spinach with just the water clinging to the leaves and the salt and stir around until it wilts. Reduce the heat to low, cover the casserole, and continue simmering until the spinach is soft.

5. Stir in the garam masala and cream, then gently return the paneer to the casserole. Simmer, stirring gently, until the paneer is heated through. Taste and adjust the seasoning, if necessary. Serve with lemon wedges for squeezing over.

Okra Stir-Fried with Onions

SERVES 4

10 oz/280 g okra

1 small red bell pepper

1 onion

2 tbsp sunflower oil or olive oil

1 tsp black or brown mustard seeds

½ tsp cumin seeds

3 large garlic cloves, lightly crushed, then chopped

½ tsp chili powder

½ tsp salt, or to taste

½ tsp garam masala

cooked basmati rice, to serve

1. Scrub each okra gently, rinse well in cold running water, then slice off the hard head. Halve diagonally and set aside.

2. Remove the seeds and core from the red bell pepper and cut into 1½-inch/4-cm strips. Halve the onion lengthwise and cut into ¼-inch/5-mm thick slices.

3. Heat the oil in a heavy-bottom skillet or wok over medium heat. When hot, but not smoking, add the mustard seeds, followed by the cumin seeds. Remove from the heat and add the garlic. Return to low heat and cook the garlic gently, stirring, for 1 minute, or until lightly browned.

4. Add the okra, red bell pepper, and onion, increase the heat to medium–high, and stir-fry for 2 minutes. Add the chili powder and salt and stir-fry for an additional 3 minutes. Add the garam masala and stir-fry for 1 minute. Remove from the heat and serve immediately with cooked basmati rice.

Mushrooms in a Rich Tomato and Onion Sauce

SERVES 4

10 oz/280 g white button mushrooms

4 tbsp sunflower or olive oil

1 onion, finely chopped

1 green chile, finely chopped (seeded if you like)

2 tsp garlic paste

1 tsp ground cumin

1 tsp ground coriander

½ tsp chili powder

½ tsp salt, or to taste

1 tbsp tomato paste

3 tbsp water

1 tbsp snipped fresh chives, for garnishing

1. Wipe the mushrooms with damp paper towels and thickly slice.

2. Heat the oil in a medium saucepan over medium heat. Add the onion and chile and cook, stirring, for 5–6 minutes, until the onion is softened but not brown. Add the garlic paste and cook, stirring, for 2 minutes.

3. Add the cumin, coriander, and chili powder and cook, stirring, for 1 minute. Add the mushrooms, salt, and tomato paste and stir until all the ingredients are blended.

4. Sprinkle the water evenly over the mushrooms and reduce the heat to low. Cover and cook for 10 minutes, stirring halfway through. The sauce should have thickened, but if it appears runny, cook, uncovered, for 3–4 minutes, or until you achieve the desired consistency.

5. Transfer to a serving dish, sprinkle the chives on top, and serve immediately.

Bombay Potatoes

SERVES 6

1 lb 2 oz/500 g new potatoes, diced

1 tsp ground turmeric

salt

4 tbsp ghee or vegetable oil

6 curry leaves

1 dried red chile

2 fresh green chiles, chopped

½ tsp nigella seeds

1 tsp mixed mustard and onion seeds

½ tsp cumin seeds

½ tsp fennel seeds

¼ tsp asafoetida

2 onions, chopped

5 tbsp chopped fresh cilantro

juice of ½ lime

1. Place the potatoes in a large, heavy-bottom pan and pour in just enough cold water to cover. Add ½ teaspoon of the turmeric and a pinch of salt and bring to a boil. Let simmer for 10 minutes, or until tender, then drain and set aside until required.

2. Heat the ghee in a large, heavy-bottom skillet. Add the curry leaves and dried red chile and cook, stirring frequently, for a few minutes, or until the chile is blackened. Add the remaining turmeric, the fresh chiles, the nigella seeds, mustard, onion, cumin and fennel seeds, and the asafoetida, onions, and fresh cilantro and cook, stirring constantly, for 5 minutes, or until the onions have softened.

3. Stir in the potatoes and cook over low heat, stirring frequently, for 10 minutes, or until heated through. Squeeze over the lime juice and serve.

Potatoes with Spiced Spinach

SERVES 4

12 oz/350 g young, waxy potatoes

9 oz/250 g spinach leaves, defrosted if frozen

3 tbsp sunflower oil or olive oil

1 large onion, finely sliced

1 fresh green chile, finely chopped (seeded if you like)

2 tsp garlic paste

2 tsp ginger paste

1 tsp ground coriander

½ tsp ground cumin

½ tsp chili powder

½ tsp ground turmeric

7 oz/200 g canned chopped tomatoes

½ tsp granulated sugar

1 tsp salt, or to taste

3 tbsp light cream

1. Cook the potatoes in their skins in a saucepan of boiling water for 20 minutes, or until tender. Drain, then soak in cold water for 30 minutes. Peel them, if you like, then halve or quarter.

2. Meanwhile, cook the spinach in a large saucepan of boiling water for 2 minutes, then drain. Transfer to a food processor and blend to a paste.

3. Heat 2 tablespoons of the oil in a medium saucepan over medium heat. Add the onion and cook, stirring, for 10–12 minutes, until browned, reducing the heat to low for the last 2–3 minutes. Remove from the heat and remove the excess oil from the onion by pressing it against the side of the saucepan with a wooden spoon. Drain on paper towels.

4. Return the pan to a low heat and add the remaining oil. Add the chile and garlic and ginger pastes and cook over low heat, stirring, for 2–3 minutes. Add the coriander, cumin, chili powder, and turmeric and cook, stirring, for 1 minute. Add the tomatoes, increase the heat to medium, and add the sugar. Cook, stirring, for 5–6 minutes.

5. Add the potatoes, spinach, salt, and reserved onion and cook, stirring, for 2–3 minutes. Stir in the cream and cook for 1 minute. Remove from the heat and serve immediately.

Garlic and Chile-Flavored Potatoes with Cauliflower

SERVES 4

12 oz/350 g young, waxy potatoes

1 head of cauliflower

2 tbsp sunflower oil or olive oil

1 tsp black or brown mustard seeds

1 tsp cumin seeds

5 large garlic cloves, lightly crushed, then chopped

1–2 fresh green chiles, finely chopped (seeded if you like)

½ tsp ground turmeric

½ tsp salt, or to taste

2 tbsp chopped fresh cilantro leaves

1. Cook the potatoes in their skins in a saucepan of boiling water for 20 minutes, or until tender. Drain, then soak in cold water for 30 minutes. Peel them, if you like, then halve or quarter according to their size—they should be only slightly bigger than the size of the cauliflower florets.

2. Meanwhile, divide the cauliflower into about ½-inch/1-cm florets and blanch in a large saucepan of boiling salted water for 3 minutes. Drain and plunge into iced water to prevent additional cooking, then drain again.

3. Heat the oil in a medium saucepan over medium heat. When hot, but not smoking, add the mustard seeds, then the cumin seeds. Remove from the heat and add the garlic and chiles. Return to a low heat and cook, stirring, until the garlic has a light brown tinge.

4. Stir in the turmeric, followed by the cauliflower and the potatoes. Add the salt, increase the heat slightly, and cook, stirring, until the vegetables are well blended with the spices and heated through.

5. Stir in the cilantro, remove from the heat, and serve immediately.

Garden Peas and Paneer in Chili-Tomato Sauce

SERVES 4

4 tbsp sunflower oil or olive oil

9 oz/250 g paneer, cut into
  1-inch/2.5-cm cubes

4 green cardamom pods, bruised

2 bay leaves

1 onion, finely chopped

2 tsp garlic paste

2 tsp ginger paste

2 tsp ground coriander

½ tsp ground turmeric

½–1 tsp chili powder

5½ oz/150 g canned chopped tomatoes

scant 2 cups warm water, plus 2 tbsp

1 tsp salt, or to taste

1¼ cups frozen peas

½ tsp garam masala

2 tbsp light cream

2 tbsp chopped fresh cilantro leaves

1. Heat 2 tablespoons of the oil in a medium nonstick saucepan over medium heat. Add the paneer and cook, stirring frequently, for 3–4 minutes, or until evenly browned. Paneer tends to splatter in hot oil, so be careful. Remove and drain on paper towels.

2. Add the remaining oil to the saucepan and reduce the heat to low. Add the cardamom pods and bay leaves and let sizzle gently for 20–25 seconds. Add the onion, increase the heat to medium, and cook, stirring frequently, for 4–5 minutes, until the onion is softened. Add the garlic and ginger pastes and cook, stirring frequently, for an additional 3–4 minutes, until the onion is a pale golden color.

3. Add the coriander, turmeric, and chili powder and cook, stirring, for 1 minute. Add the tomatoes and cook, stirring, for 4–5 minutes. Add the 2 tablespoons of warm water and cook, stirring, for 3 minutes, or until the oil separates from the spice paste.

4. Add the scant 2 cups of warm water and salt. Bring to a boil, then reduce the heat to low and simmer, uncovered, for 7–8 minutes.

5. Add the paneer and peas and simmer for 5 minutes. Stir in the garam masala, cream, and fresh cilantro and serve immediately.

Chickpeas in Coconut Milk

SERVES 4

generous 1 cup water

10 oz/280 g potatoes, cut into ½-inch/1-cm
   cubes

14 oz/400 g canned chickpeas, drained and
   well rinsed

generous 1 cup canned coconut milk

1 tsp salt, or to taste

2 tbsp sunflower oil or olive oil

4 large garlic cloves, finely chopped or crushed

2 tsp ground coriander

½ tsp ground turmeric

½–1 tsp chili powder

juice of ½ lemon

Indian bread, to serve

1. Pour the water into a medium saucepan and add the potatoes. Bring to a boil, then reduce the
   heat to low and cook, covered, for 6–7 minutes, until the potatoes are just cooked through. Add the
   chickpeas and cook, uncovered, for 3–4 minutes, until the potatoes are tender. Add the coconut
   milk and salt and bring to a slow simmer.

2. Meanwhile, heat the oil in a small saucepan over low heat. Add the garlic and cook, stirring
   frequently, until it begins to brown. Add the coriander, turmeric, and chili powder and cook, stirring,
   for 25–30 seconds.

3. Fold the aromatic oil into the chickpea mixture. Stir in the lemon juice and remove from the heat.
   Serve immediately with Indian bread.

Lentils with Cumin and Shallots
Tarka Dal

SERVES 4

1 cup red lentils

3½ cups water

1 tsp salt, or to taste

2 tsp sunflower or olive oil

½ tsp black or brown mustard seeds

½ tsp cumin seeds

4 shallots, finely chopped

2 green chiles, chopped (seeded if you like)

1 tsp ground turmeric

1 tsp ground cumin

1 fresh tomato, chopped

2 tbsp chopped fresh cilantro leaves

pilau rice, to serve

1. Wash the lentils until the water runs clear and put into a medium saucepan. Add the water and bring to a boil. Reduce the heat to medium and skim off the froth. Cook, uncovered, for 10 minutes. Reduce the heat to low, cover, and cook for 45 minutes, stirring occasionally to ensure that the lentils do not stick to the bottom of the pan as they thicken. Stir in the salt.

2. Meanwhile, heat the oil in a small saucepan over medium heat. When hot but not smoking, add the mustard seeds, followed by the cumin seeds. Add the shallots and chiles and cook, stirring, for 2–3 minutes, then add the turmeric and ground cumin. Add the tomato and cook, stirring, for 30 seconds.

3. Fold the shallot mixture into the cooked lentils. Stir in the cilantro, remove from the heat, and serve immediately with pilau rice.

Mixed Lentils with Five-Spice Seasoning

SERVES 4

generous ½ cup split red lentils (masoor dhal)

generous ½ cup skinless split mung beans (mung dhal)

3¾ cups hot water

1 tsp ground turmeric

1 tsp salt, or to taste

1 tbsp lemon juice

2 tbsp sunflower oil or olive oil

¼ tsp black mustard seeds

¼ tsp cumin seeds

¼ tsp nigella seeds

¼ tsp fennel seeds

4–5 fenugreek seeds

2–3 dried red chiles

1 small tomato, seeded and cut into strips, and fresh cilantro sprigs, to garnish

Indian bread, to serve

1. Mix both types of lentils together and wash until the water runs clear. Put them into a saucepan with the hot water. Bring to a boil, then reduce the heat slightly. Boil for 5–6 minutes, and when the foam subsides, add the turmeric, reduce the heat to low, cover, and cook for 20 minutes. Add the salt and lemon juice and beat the dhal with a wire whisk, adding a little more hot water if the dhal is too thick.

2. Heat the oil in a small saucepan over medium heat. When hot, but not smoking, add the mustard seeds. As soon as they begin to pop, reduce the heat to low and add the cumin seeds, nigella seeds, fennel seeds, fenugreek seeds, and dried chiles. Let the spices sizzle until the seeds begin to pop and the chiles have blackened. Pour the contents of the pan over the lentils, scraping off all the residue from the bottom of the pan.

3. Turn off the heat and keep the pan covered until you are ready to serve. Transfer to a serving dish and garnish with tomato strips and cilantro sprigs. Serve as a main course with Indian bread or as an accompaniment to meat, fish, or poultry dishes.

Sweet-and-Sour Lentils

SERVES 4

1¼ cups split yellow lentils (chana dal)

4 cups water

2 bay leaves, torn

3 fresh chiles, sliced once, but left whole

½ tsp ground turmeric

½ tsp ground asafoetida

3 tbsp vegetable or peanut oil

½ onion, finely chopped

¾-inch/2-cm piece fresh ginger,
  finely chopped

1 oz/30 g creamed coconut, grated

1 fresh green chile, seeded or not, to taste,
  and chopped

1½ tbsp sugar

1½ tbsp tamarind paste or tamarind chutney

½ tsp garam masala

¼ tsp ground cumin

¼ tsp ground coriander

salt

TO GARNISH

1 tbsp ghee, melted, or vegetable or peanut oil

1 tsp garam masala

chopped fresh cilantro

1. Put the lentils and water in a large pan with a lid over high heat and bring to a boil, skimming
    the surface as necessary. When the foam stops rising, stir in the bay leaves, chiles, turmeric, and
    asafoetida. Half cover the pan and let the lentils continue simmering for about 40 minutes, or until
    they are tender but not reduced to a mush, and all the liquid has been absorbed.

2. When the lentils are almost tender, heat the oil in a large, heavy-bottom pan over medium–high
    heat. Add the onion and ginger and sauté, stirring frequently, for 5–8 minutes.

3. Stir in the coconut, green chile, sugar, tamarind paste, garam masala, cumin, and coriander and stir
    for about 1 minute.

4. When the lentils are tender, add them, the bay leaves, chiles, and any liquid left in the pan to the
    spice mixture and stir around to blend together. Taste and add salt, if necessary, and extra sugar
    and tamarind, if desired.

5. Transfer the lentils to a serving dish and drizzle the hot ghee over the top. Sprinkle with garam
    masala and cilantro and serve immediately.

Kitchri

SERVES 4–6

scant 1¼ cups basmati rice
2 tbsp ghee, vegetable oil, or peanut oil
1 large onion, finely chopped
1¼ cups red split lentils (masoor dhal), rinsed
2 tsp garam masala

1½ tsp salt, or to taste
pinch of ground asafetida
3½ cups water
2 tbsp chopped fresh cilantro
chapatis and raita, to serve

1. Rinse the basmati rice in several changes of water until the water runs clear, then let soak for 30 minutes. Drain and set aside until ready to cook.

2. Melt the ghee in a flameproof casserole or large pan with a tight-fitting lid over medium–high heat. Add the onion and sauté for 5–8 minutes, stirring frequently, until golden but not browned.

3. Stir in the rice and lentils along with the garam masala, salt, and asafetida, and stir for 2 minutes. Pour in the water and bring to a boil, stirring.

4. Reduce the heat to as low as possible and cover the pan tightly. Simmer without lifting the lid for 20 minutes, until the grains are tender and the liquid is absorbed. Re-cover the pan, turn off the heat, and let stand for 5 minutes.

5. Use 2 forks to mix in the cilantro and adjust the seasoning, adding more salt if necessary. Serve with chapatis and raita.

Snacks and Accompaniments

Indians love to eat all kinds of appetizing snacks, especially before the main meal or to nibble on with drinks. Snack foods range from simple sweet and spicy nuts or plantain chips to deep-fried onion bhajis, crispy vegetable samosa triangles, and butterfly shrimp.

Also important on the Indian culinary map are the numerous breads and rice dishes that are standard accompaniments to a typical Indian meal. Breads are essential for mopping up sauces and for making meals easier to eat with the hand. They are usually unleavened and are quick and easy to make because little kneading and rising time is required. Bread appears in many forms—deep-fried pooris and crispy pappadams, oven-baked naan, grilled chapatis and parathas—all are equally delicious.

A bowl of steamed or boiled fluffy rice, delicately flavored with mild spices or coconut, is usually served with the main meal, although bread is preferred in the north. Sometimes the rice is baked in a pilau with flavorsome stock instead of water. Pilaus are lightly spiced and always include plenty of butter and tasty garnishes, such as almonds, fried onions, raisins, or golden raisins.

No Indian meal would be complete without a tray of chutneys, freshly made pickles, and cooling sauces, such as cucumber in spiced yogurt or tomato kachumbar. Not only are these served as traditional accompaniments to meat and fish dishes, but, in a land where vegetarianism is a way of life, they are an important supplement to meat-free meals.

Sweet and Spicy Nuts

SERVES 6–8

1½ cups superfine sugar

1 tsp sea salt

2 tbsp mild, medium, or hot curry powder, to taste

1 tsp ground turmeric

1 tsp ground coriander

pinch of chili powder

3 cups mixed whole blanched almonds and shelled cashew nuts

vegetable oil or peanut oil, for deep-frying

1. Mix the sugar, salt, curry powder, turmeric, coriander, and chili powder together in a large bowl, then set aside.

2. Meanwhile, bring a large pan of water to a boil. Add the almonds and cashew nuts and blanch for 1 minute, then pour them into a strainer to drain and shake off as much of the excess water as possible. Immediately toss the nuts with the sugar and spices.

3. Heat enough oil for deep-frying in a wok, deep-fat fryer, or large heavy-bottom pan to 350°F/180°C, or until a cube of bread browns in 30 seconds. Use a slotted spoon to remove the nuts from the spice mixture, leaving the spice mixture behind in the bowl, then drop the nuts into the hot oil. Cook them for 3–4 minutes, stirring occasionally and watching carefully because they can burn quickly, until they turn golden.

4. Remove the nuts from the oil with the slotted spoon and toss them in the remaining spice mixture. Pour the nuts into a strainer and shake off the excess spices, then let cool completely—they should be crispy. Store in an airtight container for up to a week.

Bhel Poori

SERVES 4

10½ oz/300 g new potatoes

7 oz/200 g canned chickpeas, rinsed and
   well drained

3½ oz/100 g sev noodles

2 oz/55 g puffed rice

4 tbsp raisins

2 tbsp chopped fresh cilantro

1 tbsp fennel seeds, toasted and cooled

pooris, crushed

salt

CHAAT MASALA

1 tbsp coriander seeds

1 tbsp cumin seeds

1 tsp black peppercorns

2 dried red chiles

TO SERVE

plain yogurt

tamarind chutney

cilantro chutney

1. Bring a large pan of salted water to a boil and cook the potatoes for 12–15 minutes, until tender. Drain and run under cold water to cool, then peel and cut into ¼-inch/5-mm dice. Cover and let chill for at least 30 minutes.

2. Meanwhile, to make the chaat masala, heat a dry skillet over high heat. Add the coriander and cumin seeds, peppercorns, and chiles and stir around until they give off their aroma. Immediately turn them out of the pan to stop them from cooking, watching closely because the cumin seeds burn quickly. Grind the toasted spice mixture in a spice grinder or with a pestle and mortar.

3. Use your hands to toss together the potatoes, chickpeas, sev noodles, puffed rice, raisins, cilantro, fennel seeds, and crushed pooris. Sprinkle with the chaat masala and toss again.

4. Divide the mixture among small serving bowls or place in one large bowl and drizzle with the yogurt and chutneys to taste. It is best eaten straight away so it doesn't become soggy.

Plantain Chips

SERVES 4

4 ripe plantains
1 tsp mild, medium, or hot curry powder,
   to taste
vegetable or peanut oil, for deep-frying
mango chutney, to serve

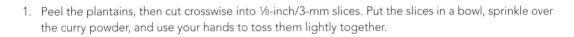

1. Peel the plantains, then cut crosswise into ⅛-inch/3-mm slices. Put the slices in a bowl, sprinkle over the curry powder, and use your hands to toss them lightly together.

2. Heat enough oil for deep-frying in a wok, deep-fat fryer, or large, heavy-bottom pan to 350°F/180°C, or until a cube of bread browns in 30 seconds. Add as many plantain slices as will fit in the pan without overcrowding and cook for 2 minutes, or until golden.

3. Remove the plantain chips from the pan with a slotted spoon and drain well on crumpled paper towels. Serve hot with mango chutney.

Spicy Onion Bhajis

SERVES 4

heaping 1 cup gram flour

1 tsp salt, or to taste

small pinch of baking soda

¼ cup ground rice

1 tsp fennel seeds

1 tsp cumin seeds

2 green chiles, finely chopped (seeded if you like)

2 large onions, about 14 oz/400 g, sliced into half rings and separated

1 cup fresh cilantro, including the tender stalks, finely chopped

scant 1 cup water

sunflower or olive oil, for deep-frying

tomato or mango chutney, to serve

1. Sift the gram flour into a large bowl and add the salt, baking soda, ground rice, and fennel and cumin seeds. Mix together thoroughly, then add the chiles, onions, and cilantro. Gradually pour in the water and mix until a thick batter is formed and all the other ingredients are thoroughly coated with it.

2. Heat enough oil for deep-frying in a wok, deep saucepan, or deep-fat fryer over medium heat to 340°–350°F/180° to 190°C, or until a cube of bread browns in 30 seconds. If the oil is not hot enough, the bhajis will be soggy. Add as many small amounts (about ½ tablespoon) of the batter as will fit in a single layer, without overcrowding. Reduce the heat slightly and cook the bhajis for 8–10 minutes, until golden brown and crisp. Maintaining a steady temperature is important to ensure that the centers of the bhajis are cooked, while the outsides turn brown. Remove and drain on paper towels. Keep hot in a low oven while you cook the remaining batter.

3. Serve hot with a tomato or mango chutney.

Crispy Vegetable Samosas

MAKES 12

3 tbsp sunflower or olive oil

½ tsp black mustard seeds

1 tsp cumin seeds

1 tsp fennel seeds

1 onion, finely chopped

2 green chiles, finely chopped (seeded if you like)

2 tsp ginger puree

½ tsp ground turmeric

1 tsp ground coriander

1 tsp ground cumin

½ tsp chili powder

2⅓ cups cubed boiled potatoes

scant 1 cup frozen peas, defrosted

1 tsp salt, or to taste

2 tbsp chopped fresh cilantro leaves

12 sheets filo dough, about 11 x 7 inches/28 x 18 cm

4 tbsp butter, melted, plus extra for greasing

chutney, for serving

1. Heat the oil in a saucepan over medium heat and add the mustard seeds, followed by the cumin and fennel seeds. Then add the onion, chiles, and ginger puree and cook, stirring frequently, for 5–6 minutes, until the onion is softened but not brown.

2. Add the ground spices and cook, stirring, for 1 minute. Add the potatoes, peas, and salt and stir until the vegetables are thoroughly coated with the spices. Stir in the cilantro and remove from the heat. Let cool completely.

3. Preheat the oven to 350°F/180°C and line a baking sheet with greased wax paper or parchment paper.

4. Place a sheet of filo dough on a board and brush well with the melted butter. Keep the remaining filo dough sheets covered with a moist cloth or plastic wrap. Fold the buttered filo dough sheet in half lengthwise, brush with some more melted butter, and fold lengthwise again.

5. Place about 1 tablespoon of the vegetable filling on the bottom right-hand corner of the filo dough sheet and fold over to form a triangle. Continue folding to the top of the sheet, maintaining the triangular shape, and moisten the ends to seal the edges. Transfer to the prepared baking sheet and brush with melted butter. Repeat with the remaining sheets of filo dough and filling.

6. Bake the samosas in the preheated oven just below the top shelf of the oven for 20 minutes, or until browned. Serve hot with chutney.

Spicy Crêpes

SERVES 6

generous ¾ cup basmati rice, soaked for 2–3 hours in cold water and drained

generous ¾ cup black lentils, soaked for 2–3 hours in cold water and drained

2 fresh green chiles, seeded and finely chopped

1 tsp dark brown sugar

salt

1¼ cups water

2 lb 12 oz/1.25 kg potatoes

3 tbsp grated fresh coconut

1-inch/2.5-cm piece fresh ginger, finely chopped

4 tbsp ghee or vegetable oil, plus extra for cooking

2 tsp black mustard seeds

2 tsp cumin seeds

1 tsp ground turmeric

3 tbsp chopped fresh cilantro

fresh cilantro sprigs, to garnish

chutney, to serve

1. Place the rice and dal in a food processor and process until ground. Pour into a bowl. Stir in half the chiles, the sugar, and a pinch of salt. Gradually add the water and mix to a smooth batter. Cover and let stand in a warm place overnight.

2. Cook the potatoes in lightly salted boiling water for 20–25 minutes, or until tender. Drain and mash. Mix the remaining chiles, coconut, and ginger to a paste.

3. Heat the ghee in a large, heavy-bottom skillet, add the mustard and cumin seeds, and stir until they give off their aroma. Stir in the coconut and ginger paste and cook for 1 minute, then add the mashed potatoes, turmeric, and cilantro and cook, stirring, for 5 minutes. Remove from the heat.

4. Heat a little ghee in an 8-inch/20-cm skillet. Stir the batter. Pour one sixth into the skillet, tilting the skillet to spread it over the bottom. Cook for 1–2 minutes, or until the underside is golden. Flip over and cook the other side for 2 minutes. Transfer to a plate and keep warm while you cook the remaining crêpes, adding more ghee as required. Divide the filling between the crêpes and fold in half. Return them to the skillet, in batches, and cook for 30 seconds on each side. Garnish with fresh cilantro sprigs and serve with chutney.

Deep-Fried Potato Balls

SERVES 4

1 lb/450 g potatoes, boiled and diced

1 onion, chopped

1-inch/2.5-cm piece fresh ginger,
   finely chopped

1 fresh green chile, seeded and finely chopped

1 tbsp chopped fresh cilantro

1 tbsp lemon juice

2 tsp aamchoor (dried mango powder)

salt

vegetable oil, for deep-frying

chutney, to serve

BATTER

¾ cup gram flour

¼ tsp baking powder

¼ tsp chili powder

salt

about ⅔ cup water

1. To make the batter, sift the flour, baking powder, chili powder, and a pinch of salt into a bowl. Gradually, stir in enough cold water to make a smooth batter. Cover with plastic wrap and set aside.

2. Place the potatoes, onion, ginger, chile, cilantro, lemon juice, and aamchoor into a separate bowl and season with salt to taste. Mix together well with a wooden spoon, breaking up the potatoes. Break off small pieces of the mixture and form into balls between the palms of your hands.

3. Heat the vegetable oil in a deep-fat fryer or heavy-bottom pan to 350–375°F/180–190°C, or until a cube of bread browns in 30 seconds. When the oil is hot, dip the potato balls in the batter, using a fork, and add to the oil, in batches. Deep-fry for 3–4 minutes, until golden brown. Remove with a slotted spoon and drain on paper towels. Keep each batch warm while you cook the remainder. Serve hot, with chutney.

Chile-Cilantro Naan

SERVES 8

3¼ cups all-purpose flour

2 tsp sugar

1 tsp salt

1 tsp baking powder

1 egg

generous 1 cup milk

2 tbsp sunflower oil or olive oil, plus extra for oiling

2 fresh red chiles, chopped (seeded if you like)

1 cup fresh cilantro leaves, chopped

2 tbsp butter, melted

1. Sift the flour, sugar, salt, and baking powder together into a large bowl. Whisk the egg and milk together and gradually add to the flour mixture, mixing it with a wooden spoon, until a dough is formed.

2. Transfer the dough to a counter, make a depression in the center of the dough, and add the oil. Knead for 3–4 minutes, until the oil is absorbed by the flour and you have a smooth and pliable dough. Wrap the dough in plastic wrap and let rest for 1 hour.

3. Divide the dough into 8 equal-size pieces, form each piece into a ball, and flatten into a thick cake. Cover the dough cakes with plastic wrap and let rest for 10–15 minutes.

4. Preheat the broiler to high. Line a broiler pan with a piece of foil and brush with oil.

5. The traditional shape of naan is teardrop, but you can make them any shape you want. To make the traditional shape, roll each flattened cake into a 5-inch/13-cm round and pull the lower end gently. Carefully roll out again, maintaining the teardrop shape, to about 9 inches/23 cm in diameter. Alternatively, roll the flattened cakes out to 9-inch/23-cm circles.

6. Mix the chiles and cilantro together, then divide into 8 equal portions and spread each on the surface of a naan. Press gently so that the mixture sticks to the dough. Transfer a naan to the prepared broiler pan and cook 5 inches/13 cm below the heat source for 1 minute, or until slightly puffed and brown patches appear on the surface. Watch carefully, and as soon as brown spots appear on the surface, turn over and cook the other side for 45–50 seconds, until lightly browned. Remove from the broiler and brush with the melted butter. Wrap in a dish towel while you cook the remaining naans.

Chapattis

MAKES 16

scant 3 cups chapatti flour (atta),
  plus extra for dusting
1 tsp salt
½ tsp sugar
2 tbsp sunflower oil or olive oil
generous 1 cup lukewarm water

1. Mix the chapatti flour, salt, and sugar together in a large bowl. Add the oil and work well into the flour mixture with your fingertips. Gradually add the water, mixing at the same time. When the dough is formed, transfer to a counter, and knead for 4–5 minutes. The dough is ready when all the excess moisture is absorbed by the flour. Alternatively, mix the dough in a food processor. Wrap the dough in plastic wrap and let rest for 30 minutes.

2. Divide the dough in half, then cut each half into 8 equal-size pieces. Form each piece into a ball and flatten into a round cake. Dust each cake lightly in the flour and roll out to a 6-inch/15-cm circle. Keep the remaining cakes covered while you are working on one. The chapattis will cook better when freshly rolled out, so roll out and cook one at a time.

3. Preheat a heavy-bottom, cast-iron grill pan or a large, heavy-bottom skillet over medium–high heat. Put a chapatti on the pan and cook for 30 seconds. Using a thin spatula, turn over and cook until bubbles begin to appear on the surface. Turn over again. Press the edges down gently with a clean cloth to encourage the chapatti to puff up—they will not always puff up, but this doesn't matter. Cook until brown patches appear on the underside. Remove from the pan and keep hot by wrapping in a piece of foil lined with paper towels. Repeat with the remaining chapattis.

Pooris

MAKES 12

1½ cups whole wheat flour, sifted,
   plus extra for dusting

½ teaspoon salt

2 tbsp ghee, melted

⅓–⅔ cup water

vegetable oil or peanut oil,
   for deep-frying

1. Put the flour and salt into a bowl and drizzle the ghee over the surface. Gradually stir in the water until a stiff dough forms.

2. Turn out the dough onto a lightly floured counter and knead for 10 minutes, or until it is smooth and elastic. Shape the dough into a ball and place it in the cleaned bowl, then cover with a damp dish towel and let rest for 20 minutes.

3. Divide the dough into 12 equal-size pieces and roll each into a ball. Working with one ball of dough at a time, flatten the dough between your palms, then thinly roll it out on a lightly floured counter into a 5-inch/13-cm circle. Continue until all the dough balls are rolled out.

4. Heat at least 3 inches/7.5 cm oil in a wok, deep-fat fryer, or large skillet until it reaches 350°F/180°C, or until a cube of bread browns in 30 seconds. Drop one poori into the hot fat and deep-fry for about 10 seconds, or until it puffs up. Use two large spoons to flip the poori over and spoon some hot oil over the top.

5. Use the two spoons to lift the poori from the oil and let any excess oil drip back into the pan. Drain the poori on crumpled paper towels and serve immediately. Continue until all the pooris are cooked, making sure the oil returns to the correct temperature before you add another poori.

Pilau Rice

SERVES 2–4

1 cup basmati rice
2 tbsp ghee
3 green cardamoms
2 whole cloves

3 black peppercorns
½ tsp salt
½ tsp saffron threads
1¾ cups water

1. Rinse the rice twice under cold running water and set aside.

2. Heat the ghee in a large, heavy-bottom pan. Add the cardamoms, cloves, and peppercorns and cook, stirring, for 1 minute. Add the rice and stir-fry for an additional 2 minutes.

3. Add the salt, saffron threads, and water to the rice mixture and reduce the heat. Cover the pan and let simmer over low heat for 20 minutes, or until all the water has evaporated.

4. Transfer the rice to a large, warmed serving dish and serve hot.

Coconut Rice

SERVES 4–6

scant 1¼ cups basmati rice
2 tbsp mustard oil

2¼ cups coconut cream
1½ tsp salt

1. Rinse the rice in several changes of water until the water runs clear, then let soak for 30 minutes. Drain and set aside until ready to cook.

2. Heat the oil in a large skillet or saucepan with a tight-fitting lid over high heat until it smokes. Turn off the heat and let the oil cool completely.

3. When you are ready to cook, reheat the oil over medium–high heat. Add the rice and stir until all the grains are coated in oil. Add the coconut cream and bring to a boil.

4. Reduce the heat to as low as possible, stir in the salt, and cover the skillet tightly. Simmer, without lifting the lid, for 8–10 minutes, until the grains are tender and all the liquid has been absorbed.

5. Turn off the heat and use two forks to mix the rice. Re-cover the pan and let the rice stand for 5 minutes.

Raita

SERVES 4–5

1 small cucumber
¾ cup whole-milk plain yogurt
¼ tsp granulated sugar
¼ tsp salt

1 tsp cumin seeds
10 to 12 black peppercorns
¼ tsp paprika

1. Peel the cucumber and scoop out the seeds. Cut the flesh into bite-size pieces and set aside.

2. Put the yogurt in a bowl and beat with a fork until smooth. Add the sugar and salt and mix well.

3. Preheat a small, heavy-bottom saucepan over medium–high heat. When the pan is hot, turn off the heat and add the cumin seeds and peppercorns. Stir around for 40–50 seconds, until they release their aroma. Remove from the pan and let cool for 5 minutes, then crush in a mortar with a pestle or on a hard surface with a rolling pin. Set aside ¼ teaspoon of this mixture and stir the remainder into the yogurt. Add the cucumber and stir to mix.

4. Transfer the raita to a serving dish and sprinkle with the reserved toasted spices and the paprika.

Tomato Kachumbar

SERVES 6

½ cup lime juice

½ tsp sugar

salt

6 tomatoes, chopped

½ cucumber, chopped

8 scallions, chopped

1 fresh green chile, seeded and chopped

1 tbsp chopped fresh cilantro

1 tbsp chopped fresh mint

1. Mix the lime juice, sugar, and a pinch of salt together in a large bowl and stir until the sugar has completely dissolved.

2. Add the tomatoes, cucumber, scallions, chile, cilantro, and mint and toss well to mix.

3. Cover with plastic wrap and let chill in the refrigerator for at least 30 minutes. Toss the vegetables before serving.

Cilantro Chutney

SERVES 4–5

1½ tbsp lemon juice

1½ tbsp water

3 oz/85 g fresh cilantro leaves and stems,
  coarsely chopped

2 tbsp chopped fresh coconut

1 small shallot, very finely chopped

¼-inch/5-mm piece fresh ginger, chopped

1 fresh green chile, seeded and chopped

½ tsp sugar

½ tsp salt

pinch of pepper

1. Put the lemon juice and water in a small food processor, add half the cilantro, and process until it is blended and a slushy paste forms. Gradually add the remaining cilantro and process until it is all blended, scraping down the sides of the processor, if necessary.

2. If you don't have a processor that will cope with this small amount, use a pestle and mortar, adding the cilantro in small amounts.

3. Add the remaining ingredients and continue processing until blended. Taste and adjust any of the seasonings, if you like. Transfer to a nonmetallic bowl, cover, and chill for up to 3 days before serving.

Mango Chutney

SERVES 4–6

1 large mango, about 14 oz/400 g, peeled, pitted, and finely chopped

2 tbsp lime juice

1 tbsp vegetable oil or peanut oil

2 shallots, finely chopped

1 garlic clove, finely chopped

2 fresh green chiles, seeded and finely sliced

1 tsp black mustard seeds

1 tsp coriander seeds

5 tbsp grated jaggery or light brown sugar

5 tbsp white wine vinegar

1 tsp salt

pinch of ground ginger

1. Put the mango in a nonmetallic bowl with the lime juice and set aside.

2. Heat the oil in a large skillet or pan over medium–high heat. Add the shallots and sauté for 3 minutes. Add the garlic and chiles and stir for an additional 2 minutes, or until the shallots are softened but not browned. Add the mustard seeds and coriander seeds, then stir.

3. Add the mango to the pan with the jaggery, vinegar, salt, and ginger and stir. Reduce the heat to its lowest setting and simmer for 10 minutes, until the liquid thickens and the mango becomes sticky.

4. Remove from the heat and let cool completely. Transfer to an airtight container, cover, and chill for 3 days before using.

Lime Pickle

SERVES 6–8

12 limes, halved and seeded
generous ⅓ cup salt
⅔ cup chili powder
¼ cup mustard powder
¼ cup ground fenugreek

1 tbsp ground turmeric
1¼ cups mustard oil
2 tbsp yellow mustard seeds, crushed
½ tsp asafetida

1. Cut each lime half into 4 pieces and pack them into a large sterilized jar, sprinkling over the salt at the same time. Cover and let stand in a warm place for 10–14 days, or until the limes have turned brown and softened.

2. Mix the chili powder, mustard powder, fenugreek, and turmeric together in a small bowl and add to the jar of limes. Stir to mix, then re-cover and let stand for 2 days.

3. Transfer the lime mixture to a heatproof bowl. Heat the oil in a heavy-bottom skillet. Add the mustard seeds and asafetida to the skillet and cook, stirring continuously, until the oil is hot and just starting to smoke.

4. Pour the oil and spices over the limes and mix well. Cover and let cool. When cool, pack into a sterilized jar. Seal and store in a sunny place for a week before serving.

Desserts and Drinks

Indian meals traditionally finish with a selection of plain fresh fruit, such as mangoes, guavas, pineapples, or melons, always carefully sliced and beautifully presented. Fruit is generally served chilled, especially in the summer months, and makes a delicious contrast to the warm, spicy main course.

Another much appreciated cooling dessert is kulfi—a type of Indian ice cream frozen in special cone-shaped molds and traditionally made by boiling milk for a long time until reduced to thick, golden, and richly flavored cream. However, it is also more quickly and easily made with evaporated milk. Kulfi may be served plain but is often flavored with saffron, mango, or coconut. It is delicious sprinkled with chopped pistachios or almonds.

On special occasions, such as a birthday, wedding, or religious feast, rich sweet desserts are served. This might be sweet saffron rice with

caramelized pineapple, or creamy shrikhand made with spiced and sweetened yogurt "cheese," garnished with jewel-like pomegranate seeds. Indians love sweet treats, such as carrot halva, which are eaten as snacks at any time of day.

With India's sky-high temperatures, there is no shortage of refreshing nonalcoholic drinks— spicy fruit juices and drinks flavored with fruit syrups, chilled mineral water or club soda flavored with ginger or lime and black pepper, or even hot milky tea served in small glasses, sometimes made fragrant with cardamom and other sweet spices. Also popular is lassi, a chilled, lightly spiced drink made with whisked yogurt diluted with water. Lassi may be sweet or salty and is served throughout India but particularly in the north, where it is popular at breakfast.

Saffron and Almond Kulfi

MAKES 4

½ tsp saffron threads

5 tbsp milk

1 tbsp ground rice

½ tbsp ground almonds

1 cup canned evaporated milk

1 cup heavy cream

2 tbsp superfine sugar

2 tbsp chopped toasted blanched almonds, to serve

1. Put the saffron threads in a dry skillet over high heat and "toast," stirring frequently until you can smell the aroma, then immediately tip them out of the pan.

2. Put the milk in the skillet over medium–high heat, add the saffron threads, and heat just until small bubbles appear around the edge. Remove the pan from the heat and let the saffron steep for at least 15 minutes. Meanwhile, combine the ground rice and ground almonds in a heatproof bowl. Put a flat freezerproof container into the freezer.

3. Reheat the milk and saffron just until small bubbles appear around the edge, then slowly beat the milk into the almond mixture, beating until it is smooth without any lumps. Pour the evaporated milk into a pan over medium–high heat and bring to a boil, stirring. Remove the pan from the heat and stir into the milk mixture. Stir in the cream and sugar.

4. Return the pan to medium heat and simmer, stirring constantly, for 5–10 minutes, until it thickens, but do not boil. Remove the pan from the heat and set aside, stirring frequently, to cool.

5. Pour the saffron mixture into the freezerproof bowl and freeze for 30 minutes, then beat to break up any ice crystals. Continue beating every 30 minutes, until the ice cream is thick and almost firm. If you are using metal kulfi molds, put them in the freezer now.

6. Equally divide the mixture among 4 kulfi molds or ramekins. Cover with the lid or plastic wrap and freeze for at least 2 hours, until solid.

7. To serve, dip a dish towel in hot water, wring it out, and rub it around the sides of the molds or ramekins, then invert onto plates. Sprinkle with the toasted almonds and serve.

Carrot Halva

SERVES 4–6

4 tbsp ghee or unsalted butter

1-inch/2.5-cm piece cinnamon stick, halved

¼ cup slivered almonds

scant ¼ cup cashew nuts

scant ¼ cup seedless raisins

8 carrots, grated

2½ cups whole milk

scant ¾ cup superfine sugar

½ tsp freshly ground cardamom seeds

½ tsp freshly grated nutmeg

¼ cup heavy cream

2 tbsp rose water

vanilla ice cream or whipped heavy cream,
  to serve

1. Melt the ghee in a heavy-bottom saucepan over low heat. Add the cinnamon stick and let sizzle gently for 25–30 seconds. Add the almonds and cashew nuts and cook, stirring, until lightly browned. Remove about 2 teaspoons of the nuts and set aside.

2. Add the raisins, carrots, milk, and sugar to the saucepan, increase the heat to medium, and bring the milk to boiling point. Continue to cook over low–medium heat for 15–20 minutes, until the milk evaporates completely, stirring frequently, and scraping and blending in any thickened milk that sticks to the side of the saucepan. Don't any milk that is stuck to the side brown or burn, because this will give the dessert an unpleasant flavor.

3. Stir in the cardamom, nutmeg, cream, and rose water. Remove from the heat and let cool slightly, then serve topped with a scoop of vanilla ice cream, with the reserved nuts sprinkled over the top.

Sweet Saffron Rice with Caramelized Pineapple

SERVES 4–6

good pinch of saffron threads, pounded

2 tbsp hot milk

scant 1 cup basmati rice

½ fresh pineapple (8 oz/225 g prepared weight)

4 tbsp ghee or unsalted butter

¾–scant 1 cup superfine sugar

4 green cardamom pods, bruised

4 cloves

2 cinnamon sticks, each ½ inch/1 cm long

1¼ cups warm water

melted butter or vegetable oil, for brushing

⅓ cup seedless raisins

scant ¼ cup toasted slivered almonds, for decorating

light cream, for serving

1. Preheat the oven to 325°F/160°C. Soak the pounded saffron in the hot milk. Wash the rice in several changes of cold water, then let drain in a colander.

2. Peel the pineapple and remove the "eyes" with a small, sharp knife. Cut the flesh into bite-size pieces. Melt 1 tablespoon of the ghee in a large, heavy-bottom skillet over low heat. Add the pineapple, sprinkle with 2 tablespoons of the sugar, and increase the heat to high. Cook, stirring, for 3–4 minutes, or until the pineapple begins to caramelize a little, then remove from the heat.

3. Melt the remaining ghee in a heavy-bottom saucepan over low heat. Add the cardamom pods, cloves, and cinnamon sticks and cook, stirring, for 25–30 seconds. Add the rice, increase the heat slightly, and cook, stirring, for 2–3 minutes. Add the saffron and milk and the warm water, bring to a boil, and boil for 2 minutes, then reduce the heat to low. Cook, uncovered, for 2–3 minutes, until the surface liquid has been absorbed by the grains. Remove from the heat.

4. Brush the sides and the bottom of a lidded ovenproof dish with a little butter and add one third of the rice. Top with one third of the raisins, followed by one third of the pineapple pieces. Sprinkle over one third of the remaining sugar evenly. Repeat this process twice more, ensuring that you finish with a layer of raisins, pineapple, and sugar.

5. Soak a piece of wax paper, crumple it, then place loosely over the top layer of fruit and sugar. Cover with a piece of foil and seal the edges by pressing it around the entire rim. Put the lid on and bake in the center of the preheated oven for 35–40 minutes. Turn off the oven and let the rice stand inside for 10–15 minutes.

6. Decorate with the slivered almonds and serve hot or cold with cream.

Indian Rice Dessert

SERVES 4

good pinch of saffron threads, pounded

2 tbsp hot milk

3 tbsp ghee or unsalted butter

heaping ½ cup ground rice

¼ cup slivered almonds

scant ¼ cup seedless raisins

2½ cups whole milk

2 cups evaporated milk

¼ cup superfine sugar

12 plumped dried apricots, sliced

1 tsp freshly ground cardamom seeds

½ tsp freshly grated nutmeg

2 tbsp rose water

TO DECORATE

¼ cup walnut pieces

2 tbsp shelled unsalted pistachios

1. Place the pounded saffron in the hot milk and let soak until needed.

2. Set aside 2 teaspoons of the ghee and melt the remainder in a heavy-bottom saucepan over low heat. Add the ground rice, almonds, and raisins and cook, stirring, for 2 minutes. Add the whole milk, increase the heat to medium, and cook, stirring, until it begins to bubble gently. Reduce the heat to low and cook, stirring frequently, for 10–12 minutes, to prevent the mixture from sticking to the bottom of the pan.

3. Add the evaporated milk, sugar, and apricots, setting a few slices aside to decorate. Cook, stirring, until the mixture thickens to the consistency of a pancake batter.

4. Add the reserved saffron-and-milk mixture, cardamom, nutmeg, and rose water, stir to distribute well, and remove from the heat. Let cool, then cover and chill in the refrigerator for at least 2 hours.

5. Melt the reserved ghee in a small saucepan over low heat. Add the walnuts and cook, stirring, until they brown a little. Remove and drain on paper towels. Brown the pistachios in the remaining ghee in the saucepan, remove, and drain on paper towels. Let the pistachios cool, then lightly crush.

6. Serve the dessert decorated with the fried nuts and the reserved apricot slices.

Shrikhand with Pomegranate

SERVES 4–6

4 cups plain yogurt
¼ tsp saffron threads
2 tbsp milk

generous ¼ cup superfine sugar, or to taste
seeds from 2 green cardamom pods
2 pomegranates or other exotic fruit

1. Line a strainer set over a bowl with a piece of cheesecloth large enough to hang over the edge. Add the yogurt, then tie the corners of the cheesecloth into a tight knot and tie them to a faucet. Let the bundle hang over the sink for 4 hours, or until all the excess moisture drips away.

2. Put the saffron threads in a dry pan over high heat and "toast," stirring frequently, until you can smell the aroma. Immediately turn them out of the pan. Put the milk in the pan, return the saffron threads, and warm just until bubbles appear around the edge, then set aside and let steep.

3. When the yogurt is thick and creamy, put it in a bowl, stir in the sugar, cardamom seeds, and saffron-and-milk mixture, and beat until smooth. Taste and add extra sugar, if desired. Cover and chill for at least 1 hour, until well chilled.

4. Meanwhile, to prepare the pomegranate seeds, cut the fruit in half and use a small teaspoon or your fingers to scoop out the seeds.

5. To serve, spoon the yogurt into individual bowls or plates and add the pomegranate seeds.

Ginger Ice Cream with Date and Tamarind Sauce

SERVES 4–5

4 cups vanilla ice cream

2 tsp ground ginger

7 oz/200 g candied ginger, chopped, to serve

TAMARIND SAUCE

⅓ cup seedless raisins

½ cup pitted dried dates

generous 1 cup boiling water

2 rounded tsp tamarind concentrate or 3 tbsp tamarind juice

scant ¼ cup molasses sugar

1. Let the ice cream stand at room temperature for 35–40 minutes to soften, then transfer to a bowl. Add the ground ginger and beat well. Return the mixture to the carton and freeze for 3–4 hours.

2. Meanwhile, to make the sauce, put the raisins and dates in a heatproof bowl, pour over the boiling water, and let soak for 15–20 minutes. Transfer to a food processor, add the tamarind and sugar, and blend to a smooth paste. Transfer to a nonmetallic bowl and let cool.

3. Put scoops of the ice cream into serving dishes and drizzle over the sauce. Arrange 2 teaspoons of candied ginger on top of each dessert and serve immediately. Serve any extra sauce separately.

Almond and Pistachio Dessert

SERVES 2

5½ tbsp unsalted butter
2 cups ground almonds
1 cup sugar

⅔ cup light cream
8 almonds, chopped
10 pistachios, chopped

1. Melt the butter in a heavy-bottom pan, preferably nonstick, stirring well. Add the ground almonds, sugar, and cream, stirring well. Reduce the heat and stir constantly for 10–12 minutes, scraping the bottom of the pan.

2. Increase the heat until the mixture turns a little darker in color.

3. Transfer the almond mixture to a large, shallow serving dish and smooth the top with the back of a spoon.

4. Decorate the top of the dessert with the chopped almonds and pistachios. Let set for 1 hour, then cut into diamond shapes and serve cold.

Salt Lassi

SERVES 4–6

3 cups plain yogurt
½ tsp salt
¼ tsp sugar
generous 1 cup water

ice cubes
ground cumin and fresh mint sprigs,
    to decorate

1. Beat the yogurt, salt, and sugar together in a pitcher or bowl, then add the water and whisk until frothy.

2. Fill 4–6 glasses with ice cubes and pour over the yogurt mixture. Lightly dust the top of each glass with ground cumin and decorate with mint sprigs.

Sweet Lassi

SERVES 4

scant 2½ cups low-fat plain yogurt
1 cup ice water
4 tbsp superfine sugar

crushed ice, to serve
finely chopped pistachios, to decorate

1. Pour the yogurt into a pitcher and whisk with a balloon whisk or hand-held electric mixer for 1–2 minutes, or until frothy.

2. Add the water and sugar and whisk until the sugar has dissolved. Pour into a pitcher, cover with plastic wrap, and let chill in the refrigerator for 30 minutes.

3. To serve, fill tall glasses with crushed ice and pour in the lassi. Sprinkle with chopped pistachios to decorate and serve immediately.

Masala Tea

SERVES 4–6

4 cups water
1-inch/2.5-cm piece fresh ginger, coarsely
    chopped
1 cinnamon stick

3 green cardamom pods, bruised
3 cloves
1½ tbsp Assam tea leaves
sugar and milk, to taste

1. Pour the water into a heavy-bottom pan over medium–high heat. Add the ginger, cinnamon stick, cardamom, and cloves and bring to a boil. Reduce the heat and simmer for 10 minutes.

2. Put the tea leaves in a teapot and pour over the water and spices. Stir and let steep for 5 minutes.

3. Strain the tea into teacups and add sugar and milk to taste.

Ginger Refresher

SERVES 4–6

¾-inch/2-cm piece of fresh ginger,
  finely chopped
½ tbsp finely grated lemon rind
5 cups boiling water

2 tbsp fresh lemon juice, or to taste
4 tbsp superfine sugar, or to taste
lemon slices and fresh mint sprigs, to decorate

1. Put the ginger in a heatproof bowl with the lemon rind. Pour over the boiling water, stir, and let steep overnight.

2. Strain the liquid into a large pitcher. Add the lemon juice and sugar, stirring until the sugar dissolves. Taste and add extra lemon juice and sugar, if you like. Serve decorated with lemon slices and mint sprigs.

Mango Cooler

SERVES 4

2 slightly underripe mangoes

4 cups ice water

4 tsp sugar

salt

crushed ice, to serve

fresh mango slices, to decorate

1. Place the mangoes in a heavy-bottom pan and add just enough water to cover. Bring to a boil, then reduce the heat, and let simmer for 10 minutes. Drain well and let cool.

2. Carefully peel off the mango skins, then, using a sharp knife, scrape the flesh away from the large central pits into a bowl.

3. Add the measured water and stir well to mix, then stir in the sugar and season with salt to taste. Stir well again, taste, and add more sugar, if necessary. Fill tall glasses with crushed ice, pour in the mango cooler, and decorate with mango slices. Serve immediately.

Index